# Contents

# Introduction

The ninth annual study conference of the United Kingdom Reading Association was held in Hamilton, near Glasgow, in August 1972. The conference theme 'The teaching of reading and related skills' reflected not only an increased awareness of the importance of acquiring competency in reading, but also a growing appreciation of the importance of 'the related skills' for both teacher and pupil.

The conference programme was organized in plenary and study sessions with some fifty contributors. Delegates were provided with abstracts of all papers on arrival at the conference. The role of the lecturer at the study sessions was to make a brief introductory statement which was meant to act as a stimulus for interchange of ideas amongst the teachers, lecturers, psychologists, advisers, inspectors, publishers and others from a wide range of disciplines attending the conference. The editors felt that the publication of these introductory statements would make for a disjointed presentation and would in no way create for those who did not attend the conference the atmosphere of active participation and interchange of ideas which characterized these sessions. For those who attended, the booklet of abstracts together with the valuable additional materials issued by many of the speakers will serve to remind them of the numerous live issues raised and of the individualistic way in which these were discussed in the different sessions.

The role of the lecturer in the plenary sessions was more formal. The papers presented are printed in these proceedings. The presidential address contains an outline of the themes covered in the conference and highlights the relevance of the papers presented. It is a source of regret that it is impossible to capture in print the conference spirit which pervaded the study and plenary sessions but it is hoped that all who read these proceedings, whether or not they attended the conference, will find something of value and that this book will take its place alongside the other UKRA conference proceedings as a contribution to 'The teaching of reading and related skills'.

Margaret M. Clark
Alastair Milne

# Part one The teaching of reading and related skills

## 1 The teaching of reading and related skills

*Margaret M. Clark*

It is valuable to be faced with an awareness of the outlook and the problems of those from other disciplines and countries; otherwise we are in danger of overemphasizing our own contribution and of failing to appreciate the extensive educational possibilities which our own school system denies us.

As *teachers*, we tend to look for solutions within the existing framework of the classroom and school. In Britain, we assume children should begin school at five years of age (or earlier) and stay until sixteen (or later). We assume that they should be in school all day and that a shortened school day is deprivation. Within schools in Scotland at least, one of our objectives is that *all* our children will be 'reading' by the age of seven, otherwise they will be at a permanent disadvantage. To what extent is any disadvantage the inevitable consequence, or merely the result of our particular school approach to education and school organization, or our failure to cater for children's varied needs and individual rates of development? While seeking our short-term solutions within the present educational system, we should look beyond that in our evaluation of its long-term effectiveness.

We should look to other countries to see whether we are perhaps too much concerned with amount of time spent in school and too little concerned with the quality of the provision. We should look to other agencies to see whether we perhaps overvalue the role of the teacher in education and underestimate the potential role of the parent or the teaching aide. We should look to other materials and media to see whether we overstress the part played by educationally accepted books and materials in the *teaching* of reading and undervalue the potential of other materials and media in *learning* to read.

If as *college of education lecturers* we meet only others with a similar background, we may well seek to extend the initial training of teachers, claiming that only then can the training be adequate in imparting all the knowledge that the student is expected to acquire, forgetting perhaps that some aspects of competence can most successfully be taught in-service; some can be taught in no other way. Perhaps we attempt to pack too much into preservice training. This is particularly unfortunate in a field where knowledge is not static but a growing and developing body of understanding. Were we, in teaching, dealing with a body of facts to be acquired by the intending teacher and passed on to the expectant young child, perhaps there might be justification for such a course. In reading, we have no evidence that there *is* one right way, or a body of 'facts' to pass on to the intending teacher. Indeed, we may well be at a breakthrough in the understanding of the teaching of reading—but too late for those now entering the schools. Should we be at such a point, colleges can help only by encouraging students towards a critical appraisal of new developments by analysis of existing practices rather than by encouraging uncritical acceptance of an existing body of knowledge, no matter how extensive.

As *psychologists* we need, at least as much as anyone, to discuss with others the developments in the teaching of reading. Psychologists, by the nature of their professional involvement, tend to be preoccupied with the failures in reading. Apart from studies of the relative effectiveness of various competing methods or media as the best approach to the initial teaching of reading, research has concentrated on children who have failed in reading. Studies have focussed on the visual and auditory perception, intelligence, language and home background of such children—and more recently the school background of those who have failed to learn to read. Important factors contributing to success in reading may fail to be appreciated if we study only the failures. The characteristics of the successful reader are worthy of investigation to illuminate our understanding of reading as a form of communication. Such study should, in addition, lead us to a more accurate perception of the role of various deficits as causal factors in reading failure; we may find indeed that some fluent readers are highly successful in spite of such disabilities.

Another topic which has attracted a great deal of attention is the measurement of the percentages of nonreaders at seven or eleven or fifteen years of age with comparisons of these in different areas or countries, or at different times. These studies have been coupled with controversy as to whether the percentages are different now from previously and whether they are becoming or will become higher with 'progressive' methods. This dichotomy of those who can and those who cannot read carries with it the implicit assumption that teaching children to read is an all or none process; that it is the concern of the teachers in the early part of the school and that subsequent teachers are mainly involved in dealing with those with whom the initial teaching or the teachers have failed. The role of the psychologist is then to intervene when all the teachers have failed. The teacher's conception of the psychologist as the person involved in reading surveys and in the testing of children's reading progress is an unfortunate one, made more so by the limited testing instruments which have been available in this country.

Comparative studies of standards of children at seven years of age are more dangerous than valuable. Within even an area or a county, a global figure may be dangerous if treated in isolation, as so often happens. Does it matter if some children cannot read at seven? If it does, why? Are they not reading because of a conscious policy to delay reading instruction and extend the period of oral communication, or are they failing in spite of a conscious policy of instruction? There is a place and an important place for assessment in the teaching of reading. If, however, testing does not lead to action and more effective action, then the time spent on testing could indeed more profitably have been spent on teaching. Some teachers' distrust of tests is unfortunate but understandable. The feeling of some teachers and some psychologists that the testing of reading progress is the prerogative of the psychologist is even more unfortunate. For many teachers, tests of reading progress are synonymous with Burt, Vernon or Schonell, with identification of words in isolation, and with results in terms of reading ages. It is not so much that some tests are 'bad' and some 'good', but rather a matter of knowing the range of tests, their limitations and values and of selecting the appropriate test for one's purpose. The professional role of the psychologist in the field of assessment is as the consultant who is aware of the range of assessment techniques available, their limitations and purposes, and who is both ready and able to meet with his teacher colleagues to discuss the problem involved and to advise.

There have been two recent indications of a move towards the co-ordination of action between psychologists and teachers which is advocated here.

First, the recommendation in the Tizard Report *Children with Specific Reading Difficulties* (DES 1972) that:

(i) in collaboration with educational psychologists and school medical officers, teachers should screen all children for reading backwardness, preferably at the end of the infant stage
(ii) both schools and educational psychologists should maintain a continuing check for as long as necessary on the subsequent progress of children identified as backward in reading.

Such screening would provide a school with an 'at risk' register in educational terms. All children identified as failing at seven years of age would not necessarily require specialist treatment but the schools would be alerted to their existence and their progress could then be monitored from an early age. It is hoped that these recommendations will be *encouraged* rather than adopted wholesale so that they grow out of an increasing competence on the part of teachers in the field of assessment and a growing relationship between psychologists and teachers with regard to the diagnostic teaching of reading.

The second illustration is the publication this year of the first of the *Edinburgh Reading Tests* (1972). These tests are being developed for use by classroom teachers as a result of requests from Scottish teachers through their teachers' organization. The tests have been planned by an interdisciplinary steering committee of test constructors, psychologists, college lecturers and representatives of the teaching profession. That the tests will be criticized I am sure; that they will be modified and developed in the light of experience I also feel confident. It is not sufficient that standardized test procedures are utilized. Informal inventories of children's progress are also required, indicating their weaknesses and their strengths. Here again we can hope that teachers, psychologists and advisers will all be involved. Recording progress is all the more important, the more individualized and informal the approach to the teaching of reading. The need for some common policy over at least a local area is seen from the evidence not only of frequent changes of staff within a school, but also frequent changes of school by many children. One in four children in my study in Dunbartonshire changed school at least once within the first two years (Clark 1970) and the figure for Scotland, England and Wales is quoted as 17 per cent (Davie, Butler and Goldstein 1972).

In Scotland, there is a tendency to be complacent about achievements in the field of reading and the related skills. We have watched as our colleagues in the English colleges of education were subjected to a government enquiry—the James Report *Teacher Education and Training* (DES 1972). As this did not apply to Scotland, we could read with interest but without concern, prepared, I hope, to select those aspects of relevance to our own scene.

Our colleagues in the schools in England have been the subject of several recently published studies. In *The Roots of Reading* (Cane and Smithers 1971) the standards of achievement in schools in the London area with more and less formal approaches to the teaching of reading were compared. Higher standards were associated with schools with 'firmer' attitudes and more 'formal' teachers and this finding has been greeted with pleasure by those who disapprove of the child-centred approach and favour a return to a more formalized instruction. It should be borne in mind, however, that the study was carried out in 1959 to 1961 although the report was pubished in 1971. This is relevant to any discussion of cause and effect as is the following quotation:

> ...that there were exceptions to this norm and that the most successful school of all (Godwin) was one which combined activity methods and creativity with a certain amount of teacher direction, especially in organizing the learning of phonics.

More recently the National Foundation for Educational Research published the results of a national survey entitled *The Trend of Reading Standards* (Start and Wells 1972) based on a study of reading standards in eleven and fifteen year olds (who began school in 1964 and 1961 respectively). It was found in England and Wales 'that reading standards today are no better than they were a decade ago'. As a result of that enquiry, the Minister of Education has set up a committee to consider in relation to schools, (i) all aspects of teaching the uses of English including reading, writing and speech; (ii) how present practice might be improved, and the role that initial and in-service teacher training might play; (iii) to what extent arrangements for monitoring the general level of attainment in these skills could be introduced or improved. On this committee are the three most recent past presidents of UKRA—Keith Gardner, John Merritt and Vera Southgate—an indication of the recognition being accorded to the UKRA as an influence in improving the standards of reading and the related skills.

The most recent national survey in Scotland, undertaken by the Scottish Council for Research in Education, made a comparison of standards in English and arithmetic of the ten year olds in 1953 and 1963 entitled *Rising Standards in Scottish Primary Schools 1953–1963* (Scottish Council for Research in Education 1968). No further comparison will be based on the same tests since 'in view of changes now taking place in the curriculum of the primary school, it is evident that the tests used in this survey cannot be used in any future survey'. However this year in Scotland, a new research has just begun in which a study will be undertaken into the relationships between standards of reading and classroom practice over three age groups.

To encourage Scottish complacency about the teaching of reading still further, it is stated in the national comparisons of attainment (Davie, Butler and Goldstein 1972) which formed part of the interdisciplinary study of children of seven years of age, that:

In reading attainment the most striking feature to emerge from the results is that the proportion of good readers in Scotland is markedly higher than in any other region of Britain. This difference is even more marked for poor readers . . . for every eighteen poor readers in Scotland there were proportionately twenty-nine poor readers in England and thirty in Wales.

A further study of these children has been carried out at eleven years of age on a test of reading comprehension and it is not yet known whether the Scottish children have held this lead in reading attainment. Certainly one comparative study of Scottish, English and American children (Anderson 1966) indicated that it was only in spelling that the Scottish children retained their lead by school leaving age.

7

The early start in the teaching of reading, the systematic instructional techniques and the tendency towards a more phonically based approach would all help Scottish children to perform well on a task which involved word identification from a selection of alternatives. Such a test while designed for, and indeed useful for, identifying children who have failed to make a start in reading at the end of the infant stage, is scarcely an adequate measure of 'good' reading. For that reason, the statement quoted above is perhaps misleading in its implications. Clearly from this study and other evidence there are only a limited number of children in Scotland who have not acquired the basic skill of word identification after two years at school (Clark 1970). What proportion of these children are 'good' readers at seven years of age or indeed later is a very different question. Learning to read should not be regarded as a hierarchy of skills from lower to higher order but as a developmental language process where the approaches in the initial stages will colour the children's motivation and their perception of reading as a purposeful and valuable activity. Only if on completing their schooling our Scottish children show themselves as *able* to read with comprehension for a variety of purposes and *willing* to read, can we feel confident in the success of our teaching. It may be that an early and systematic start is *the* or *a* successful basis on which to build—this we have yet to determine.

Is the task of the school only the more efficient teaching of the basic skills and the provision thereafter of an enriched environment with an adequate supply of books and the need to consult them? Probably this is only true where the teaching of reading in its fullest sense is being achieved by the environment provided by the parents—the language, the motivation and the materials compensating for the inadequacy of the schools. Perhaps as educationists we are too ready to accept credit for the successes and to attribute the failures to the parents. We can never know how many of the children who read critically and purposefully after attending school would have read effectively had they been at home. The term 'compensatory education' is unfortunate in its implied condemnation of the home. It is important that we consider not only the role of the entire school in the development of reading and the related skills, but also that we give due appreciation to the contribution and the potential contribution of the parents to the education process. In school and preschool education, we perhaps overvalue the specialist and undervalue the contribution of the parents—and with that the skills brought by the child to the learning situation. Parents are being made to feel less and less adequate. Even the plea for nursery education for all has an implied criticism of parental competence; particularly coupled with our reluctance as specialists to allow the parents more than a peripheral role—even in preschool education. Perhaps our attitude towards the parents is a reflection of our own present insecurity and uncertainty concerning our role in a society changing at such a speed that what seems important today may no longer be relevant tomorrow.

Just as we are in danger of undervaluing the role of the parents, so also we are in danger of failing to appreciate the characteristics which the child brings to the reading task (Smith 1971):

> Two things are perhaps surprising about the skills and knowledge that a child brings with him when he is about to learn to read: the sheer quantity and complexity of his ability, and the small credit that he is usually given.

'Reading readiness' as a concept with its emphasis on the inadequacies of the child, tends to reassure the insecure teacher that the failures were not hers but the child's. His poor visual discrimination, auditory discrimination, motor coordination or his language were inadequate. There must be few characteristics measured in any test of reading readiness which are absolute barriers to learning to read. Some may make a particular technique or group situation inappropriate. The child with poor auditory discrimination may find it more difficult to learn by a phonically based approach—particularly if the classroom is noisy; and the child with poor visual discrimination may have his difficulties increased by a look-say approach—particularly if the teacher's writing is not clear; while the child with limited grasp of language may have problems if the teacher's explanations are predominantly verbal. It is salutary, however, to bear in mind the child described by Krippner (1963) who would clearly have failed a test of reading readiness but at the age of three was already a fluent reader.

Readiness of the *school* for the child should now receive as much attention as has previously been given to the readiness of the child for the school.

In an ongoing study of children who were already fluent readers when they started school, I have been impressed by a number of interesting aspects of the development of their fluent reading which might not have occurred to me had I confined my attention only to children who had learned to read in the school group situation. One aspect which worries me considerably is the parents' embarrassment that they have sent their child to school able to read. Why should we make parents feel guilty if their child comes to school able to read and ashamed if he comes not ready to read?

Not all children in my present study are highly intelligent; not all their parents are in the professional classes. Indeed, not all had a range of interesting and stimulating children's books for their first experiences of printed material and certainly few had any structured reading scheme. Unlikely materials like car numbers, the daily newspaper, the *Radio Times*, an old pack of lexicon cards and even the television advertisements had acted as a stimulus to these children. One important common factor for these children seems to have been an interested, though not necessarily well-informed, adult. One important characteristic of these children is their awareness of what they can and cannot do.

As Smith (1971) stated so forceably in *Understanding Reading:*

> A clearer understanding of what the skilled reader can do, and of what the beginning reader is trying to do, is far more important for the reading teacher than any revision of instructional materials.
>
> The 'decoding' that the skilled reader performs is not to transform visual symbols into sound, which is the widely held conventional view of what reading is about, but to transform the visual representation of language into meaning.

The child, when he starts to read, does not require to be taught language but the written representation of language. He does not have to be taught to look; he has to be taught the significant characteristics of print. He needs to know *enough*, not all, about the letters. Fluent reading does not necessitate a minute analysis of each aspect of each letter or word but only sufficient to extract meaning from the printed page. A large number of interrelated skills developed over a period of years are necessary for reading. Ability to recall nonsense syllables does not differentiate good and poor readers. If, to quote Merritt (1970) 'the ability to anticipate sequences is the basis of fluent reading' then a willingness to make mistakes is likely to be part of the process of learning to read. 'Guessing' is only bad for a child if it is based on wrong cues. It may be, however, a stage in the development of linguistic competence leading to fluent reading. The child has to discover the distinctive features of print, of words and of letters, and the teacher must, in order to assist in this development, provide not only examples, but contrasts. She must herself be aware of the significance of the various characteristics of language and of print. When, for example, we talk of two letters being 'the same' or 'different', what do we mean? The child must learn by response and by feedback from the teacher or another adult. This appears to have been one of the roles that the parents played for the precocious readers referred to earlier. Many of these children initiated the situation but the parents confirmed the hunch or suggested the alternative when the child could not otherwise make sense of the reading material. Some of the recent studies of children's concept formation have again appeared to reinforce the feeling of the children's inadequacies. One must, however, distinguish a child's ability to solve a problem from his ability to verbalize his solution. In her recent study of children's concepts of reading, Reid (1966) indicated the limited appreciation in many five year old children of the distinction between, for example, a letter, a word and a number. Let us not be misled, however, into teaching the children only to verbalize the concepts. Even many of the fluent readers at five years of age could not verbalize the concepts but they certainly had some appreciation of them. Let us not underestimate a child's understanding because of his inability to describe his solution, for as Brandis and Henderson (1970) have pointed out:

> It is unlikely that working class children do not possess in their passive vocabulary the middle class range of adjectival, noun and verb types ... it is even more unlikely that middle class and working class children differ in terms of their tacit understanding of the linguistic rule system ... it is more the case that there is a difference in the social function of language.

Too little consideration may be given in schools to the justification which a child could, if asked, advance for his particular solution to a problem; equally, too much emphasis may be laid on the choice of the appropriate language when we assess a child's understanding of concepts. Some children may be both underestimated and further deprived in schools by our emphasis on a precision in language for the purpose of explanation by teacher and child in the early stages. Teaching based rather on significant examples and contrasts might better encourage some children to develop their own rule systems. In the field of reading, one example of this would be instances of similarities and differences as these terms apply to the distinction between letters or words rather than a verbal explanation of these distinctions in terms which may be confusing to some children. Simultaneously, a programme to broaden the children's active language experiences could sensitize them to the variety of language structures. In *Talk Reform*, Cahagan and Cahagan (1970) describe their attempts, with the assistance of infant teachers, to devise such a programme whose aim was to help the children develop a language of registers appropriate for different occasions, and not to make them suppress their 'incorrect speech' and substitute 'correct' (middle class) speech.

Just as purpose, and purpose seen by the child, is important as a motivating force in learning to read, so purpose in writing is important in written communication. This gives point to the teaching of handwriting and spelling as aspects of written communication since both are tools for written communication. As Peters (1967) has shown, though spelling can be caught by some, it can also be taught and most effectively when the instruction is systematically organized, taking into account the linguistic probabilities of the English language and the child's needs in written communication.

If we wish to develop literacy in all children, then we must proceed developmentally from oral communication for a purpose in a wide range of contexts to an integrated approach to reading and writing. If one considers the extent to which children, even from so-called deprived homes, are bombarded with speech, one appreciates that their difficulties arise not from lack of speech, but lack of communication. No language programme will succeed in which the children are the passive recipients of the teacher's speech, no matter how stimulating and varied, unless this leads in turn to wide and varied participation by the children themselves. As Merritt (1970) says:

> What could be less motivating than the repeated setting down of the obvious for the already well-informed ... the critical feature in developing communication skills (is) the opportunity to communicate with an array of different recipients on a variety of subjects in a variety of contexts.

If an educated man is defined as one who has acquired the ability to listen thoughtfully, to speak effectively, to read critically and to write creatively, are these realistic aims for the teaching of reading and the related skills? If so, for whom? For only a chosen few or for all but a small minority? Our professional competence will determine the answer.

## References

ANDERSON, I. H. (1966) Comparisons of the reading and spelling achievements and quality of handwriting of groups of English, Scottish and American children *Cooperative Research Projects No 1903* Michigan: University of Michigan

BRANDIS, W. and HENDERSON, D. (1970) *Social Class, Language and Communication* London: Routledge and Kegan Paul

CANE, B. and SMITHERS, J. (1971) *The Roots of Reading* Slough: National Foundation for Educational Research

CLARK, M. M. (1970) *Reading Difficulties in Schools* Harmondsworth: Penguin

DAVIE, R., BUTLER, N., and GOLDSTEIN, H. (1972) *From Birth to Seven* London: Longman

DES (1972) *Children with Specific Reading Difficulties* (Tizard Report) London: HMSO

DES (1972) *Teacher Education and Training* (James Report) London: HMSO

*Edinburgh Reading Tests* (1972) London: University of London Press

GAHAGAN, D. M. and GAHAGAN, G. A. (1970) *Talk Reform: Exploration in Language for Infant School Children* London: Routledge and Kegan Paul

KRIPPNER, S. (1963) The boy who read at eighteen months *Exceptional Children* November, 105–109

MERRITT, J. (1970) Teaching reading in junior and secondary schools in *Teaching Reading: Ace Forum 4* London: Ginn

PETERS, M. L. (1967) *Spelling: Caught or Taught?* London: Routledge and Kegan Paul

REID, J. F. (1960) Learning to think about reading *Educational Research* 9, 1, 56–62

SCOTTISH COUNCIL FOR RESEARCH IN EDUCATION (1968) *Rising Standards in Scottish Primary Schools 1953–1963* London: University of London Press

SMITH, F. (1971) *Understanding Reading* New York: Holt, Rinehart and Winston

START, K. B. and WELLS, B. K. (1972) *The Trend of Reading Standards* Slough: National Foundation for Educational Research

# Part two Research implications and applications

## 2 Reading research from the outside and the inside

*John G. Morris*

This year is particularly appropriate for considering research in education in this country, since the Government issued in 1971 the Rothschild Report, *A Framework for Government Research and Development* (Civil Service Department 1971) which has led to a host of position papers from interested institutions, a report from the Select Committee on Science and Technology (1971) dealing with research and development, and more letters to *The Times* than any other event since the claim of the first man to have heard the voice of the cuckoo abroad in the land. The two are not unconnected. Broadly the Rothschild Report wanted research with practical results, which could point up the way for policy-making and spoke of a customer-contractor relationship and of consumer-oriented research.

All this is in an area of endeavour called education, which in the United Kingdom spends about £5,000 per minute, but very little on research. When we look at the input in terms of personnel we find that no matter whose name is on the application form for a research grant, the leg-work is being done by someone young, usually female, often poorly paid, and although well-educated yet rather inexperienced, in a field which values experience beyond rubies. Fortunately the freshness of inexperience is so stimulating.

Proposals for projects to fund-granting bodies tend to be dull and pedestrian, sometimes not very clearly planned, and foredoomed to produce results which will not be very exciting but more likely to produce from teachers and others the reaction, 'so what?'. When compared with the research effort available in science, engineering and medicine, education is light-years behind.

Let us now begin to use a smaller brush and consider research in reading.

Someone with more time on his hands than sense in his head has calculated that there are some 29,000 different research projects reported on reading. Classification of them is difficult, as it is in all research, but a brief survey of the various research registers shows that methods, schemes, practices and disability account for most of the projects. How teachers are taught to teach reading in their training courses, and what makes a good reader, seem to be relatively unworked ground.

This paper considers the point of view of the outsider and the insider, and these terms themselves indicate an attitude, and are interchangeable. For my purpose the teacher is the insider. He or she used to be called the person at the coal-face, and we still use this rather dusty and dated metaphor in a nuclear age. Such is the conservatism of educational thought. Contact with teachers leaves me with the impression that many of them are beset by doubts because of lack of success with certain pupils, and some of them seem more worried about the backward pupils than these backward pupils themselves. As they are looking for help one would expect them to be potentially ready to accept research findings.

Contact with research workers leaves me with the impression that they would like to do something practical and produce findings which could be implemented—preferably in the raw state. Thus the two groups would seem to be similarly motivated to such a degree that they should mesh, but often they do not. Let us consider possible constraints which apply to the research worker and to the teacher, under the headings of objectives, instruments and conclusions.

*Objectives*
There are people who have an attitude of mind which enables them to sit down and plan what they want to do, then plot the steps towards it. Teachers in training, even at the beginning of this century, were told about the goal-seeking animals and insects by psychologists. A favourite in Scotland was caterpillars walking round a flower-pot rim—they were still walking in 1946 but by then the flower-pots were plastic. The students as ever dismissed it as irrelevant. Programmed learning also made great play with the need to state objectives before writing the programme, and the revival of behaviourism by Skinner led to the demand that the objectives should be stated in behavioural terms. This way of thinking spread to other fields, not only educational ones. For example management became a science and 'management by objectives' enjoyed a good run. Some tremendous commonplaces were mouthed, from 'getting our priorities right' to the elementary advice of sifting through the mail and dealing with the important items first. What climber decides to cut his teeth on Mount Everest?

Teachers of reading could decide on objectives but there were two kinds of doubt. One was the temptation in any classroom to identify what is going for you as the teacher and make that the objective. The other was the reasonable doubt, especially held by some teachers of infants, that objectives got in the way of learning. If creativity and activity and discovery were desirable features in a learning environment, then objectives would become major and unacceptable constraints. Apocryphal tales arose of teachers who did their educating in the mornings and their projects in the afternoons. Another story was about two small boys in the playground discussing the thrust problem of a passing jet aircraft and then resignedly returning to school to 'string more of them damned beads'. My favourite is that of the teacher who timetabled 'creativity' for 3 to 4 p.m. every afternoon, except Tuesday. Most of these stories are made up by teachers themselves—at least testifying to their insight.

*Instruments*

The outsider, the research worker, in this environment has to decide how he can use instruments which will not be at variance with the desired objectives of the teacher. Worse, he has to do it in a number of schools and lump his results together to produce quantifiable data with a large N, as this is respectable in research circles, although people like Piaget, and Spearman before him, had got away with small numbers. Almost without exception the research worker's background is one where he has prepared a thesis for degree purposes showing that he understood research design, and could apply statistical procedures to the results—even if they were not always relevant procedures.

An area of common ground for teachers and research workers is that they both use instruments. Unfortunately they are not the same instruments. I have alluded to one above for the research worker, that of statistics. In a population which is not particularly numerate it is understandable that statistics will cause concern, but it is unforgivable that they should be used to overwhelm and even to browbeat. If the choice is between good and bad data, and good and bad statistics, the only acceptable selection is good data and bad statistics. You can do nothing with bad data, and statistics will not improve them. On the other hand the teacher's complaint that you can prove anything by statistics has to be rejected. You can prove nothing by statistics, only show trends; that is what statistics are for.

The other instruments of the research worker are questionnaires and tests. Both look deceptively simple and unimpressive. There is a firm belief that any fool can draw up a questionnaire—many do! There is only one way to produce a test and that is by slow pilot work, with many drafts and validation on an appropriate population. There are teachers who do not see the need for standardization of tests and are unwilling to consider relative as opposed to absolute values which they may call 'standards', and which they recognize unerringly by using a touchstone called experience. It is just possible to discuss and even argue with them. The more difficult teachers to have a discussion with are the ones who say that the test is all very well, but that it does not measure what is important, and even that what is important is an imponderable and cannot be measured. In that case how do they know it is there? Any test construction must proceed against an agreed analysis of what is important, what is specific and what is possible in the area being tested. It must also be matched against the practical situation of crowded classrooms, teachers with wide-ranging rather than deep skills, children with a limited span of attention, and that host of instant problems which make up the school day.

As I have said, teachers too use instruments. The first is the graded book even if at the level that page seven is an advance on page six, and that the child on page seven has therefore progressed. Now much more sophisticated books are available which have been constructed with patient research, using vocabulary counts, levels of word difficulty— single words, or phrases, or idiom. Some of the most useful work has provided checklists to enable the teacher to go to a daunting book exhibition, set up by publishers at some conference, with a greater degree of purpose than the aimless flick through the pages.

Another of the instruments for teachers has the rather grandiose title of a multimedia kit. In fact this is usually reading material, work cards or response sheets, and support material in the form of slides, pictures and audio-tape. At present it seldom has moving picture facilities in the form of film or television clips, whether cassette-loaded or not. This instrument is seldom used at the early stages of the school, but is needed once reading as a tool skill has been established, so that progress in reading can take place. The research worker is usually involved in the production of the kit, as material which is expensive to produce must be tried out to see if it works. The teachers may have reservations about the material, claiming that it is too structured and cramps the creativity of the individual pupil. Once we move away from the mechanics of teaching reading and into learning activity based on skill in using reading, we are on much less sound ground when speaking about progress and development.

The third instrument for the teacher is something which indicates progress. Even the most avant garde teacher, way out at the frontiers of development, has to stop and ask at times whether what she is doing is effective and whether pupils are progressing. You can resist tests, object to schemes of work and condemn profiles and even prevaricate to the extent of saying: 'It all depends on what you mean by "progress" ' (Joad, thou shouldst be living at this hour!) but you must decide that you are either a teacher, or an involuntary spectator at a happening, or at least somewhere on the continuum joining these two points. To teach at all is to interfere to some extent, and having done so you must consider the effect.

Word recognition tests and further material of the Schonell type were once eagerly used by teachers, but part of the fashion now is to decry what does not deal with imponderables. Of course word recognition tests were blunt instruments, but they were quick and easy to use and gave the teacher an instrument, beyond that of her own judgment, which would be highly reliable at the extremes, but inevitably less reliable as she approached the mean. The demand from teachers in Scotland, as expressed through their own institute (the Educational Institute of Scotland) is for a quick, reliable method of assessing progress which has analysed needs, has some degree of sophistication, can be used on groups, is easy to score and interpret and provides diagnostic indicators. This is the egg-laying pig that gives wool and milk—a rare animal! Let us move out of the classroom again into the wider area and consider some conclusions.

### Conclusions

There is pressure from the teacher on the research worker to be practical and relevant, and pressure from society to ensure that the customer gets what he wants. The Rothschild Report puts the needs of society high on its list. Society is only one man thick. A parent wants his child to read well and be successful at school. An employer wants his employees to be competent. Of course it is pleasant if other children can read too, and if other employees are able—but not essential to society as seen through one pair of eyes.

The research worker needs to have a minimum level of sophistication if he is going to be judged competent by his peer group, and this will affect his career prospects. Further he has to satisfy too many masters, some of whom have highly developed disciplines of their own, and he is not a polymath. Sociologists who seldom use the adjective 'educational' in front of their name, and philosophers and psychologists who often do, insist on consideration being given to variables from their disciplines. Administrators, policy makers and teachers demand unequivocal positive statements. Research design involves problems of variables such as the varying skills of teachers independent of methods and the essential rights of pupils in any control group. We end up with a careful piece of work which shows that if a child is born in summertime, has many brothers and sisters, suffers from physical, auditory or visual defects, has parents who have separated, lives in a restricted environment, lacks experiences and the stimulus of talk with adults, and has a substandard house in a working class area with a high degree of unemployment, he will be a backward reader. Probably the most crucial question for the teacher to answer is 'Given all these in a child or children do I just deplore the fates and say, "Alack the day" or do I seek salvation through materials and methods?' Such a child does not need support—he needs a miracle, but miracles do happen.

In summary then you have two groups of people with common yet vague objectives, crude instruments with which to work, and a degree of mutual mistrust, each group seeing its own problems writ large, and working in a social milieu which makes demands upon but does not particularly like either group, and judges educational performance primarily by a single touchstone, which is the raison d'être for this conference and this association—reading. It is so humiliating and restricting to be unable to read. The two groups can be mutually reinforcing and reassuring.

*References*

CIVIL SERVICE DEPARTMENT (1971) *A Framework for Government Research and Development* (Rothschild Report) London: HMSO

SELECT COMMITTEE ON SCIENCE AND TECHNOLOGY: 1971 *Second Report: Research Councils* London: HMSO

# 3 The problem of evaluating aids to the teaching of reading in schools

*Alan Little and Janet Woods*

## Why evaluate?

Although the importance of children learning to read has never been questioned, it is only in recent years that teachers have been faced with a multitude of theories, techniques and audio-visual aids by which the skill of reading is said to be acquired and developed. New reading schemes have appeared on the market, theories of whether reading is caught or taught have been expounded and a mass of audio-visual aids such as the Talking Page, the Language Master, the Audio Page and the Science Research Associates and Ward Lock Educational reading laboratories have appeared. Schools and local education authorities are constantly faced with publicity concerning these new techniques for which the claims usually made are that they are the answer to all the teachers' problems. The schools and authorities, however, have to decide whether they should adopt the new methods or whether they should provide the money to purchase such equipment and, once purchased, for which children it is likely to be most suitable. They therefore need to evaluate the equipment, first because of the primary importance of the acquisition of reading skills by all children, and second because the misuse of techniques or the use of the wrong techniques may not only fail to help the children but may in fact harm them. In addition the cost of equipment is high and the scarcity of resources means that the optimum use needs to be made of the resources that are available.

## The style of the evaluation

### Rigidly controlled versus 'real-life' studies

Audio-visual aids and other teaching techniques can be evaluated under various conditions. A situation similar to that frequently used in the natural sciences can be adopted with carefully controlled experimental and control groups or the equipment can be evaluated in the 'real-life' teaching situation of the school. In the former case it is the 'potentiality' of the equipment or curriculum innovation that will be established by the evaluation; in the latter it is its efficacy in the normal school situation. However, in the natural sciences the variables involved can be more rigidly controlled than they can in education, e.g. children cannot be totally matched so that two groups are identical with each other and even when matching to an acceptable degree has taken place, this does not ensure that in all other aspects except that of the new technique the learning experience of the children is identical. Each group may have a different teacher or even if the same teacher takes both groups, she may have different attitudes to each group or to the different learning techniques. The methods of research adopted must depend on who requires the research and for what purpose.

The interest group requiring the research
Whoever initiates the research has to decide which form of evaluation is most appropriate to the questions which he wishes to have answered. If the evaluators are the manufacturers their main aim is to sell the equipment. If the evaluators are schools or an education authority, i.e. potential purchasers of the equipment, the effects of the equipment when introduced into the ordinary school situation will be most important. If the evaluators are academics with no interest in either selling or buying the machine or learning system their main interest is likely to be in the potentiality of the system or in very specific learning areas, depending on the problems they are considering.

This paper is particularly concerned with evaluation from the point of view of the purchaser—the school or education authority. It is therefore mainly concerned with the problem of evaluating teaching aids in the classroom—the situation in which the equipment will eventually be used. Illustrations have been taken from two projects undertaken by the authors for the Inner London Education Authority—a study of Rank's Talking Page and a study of the Science Research Associates' Reading Laboratories.

*Defining the objectives*
Although the aims laid down by the manufacturers may be very specific, for example Rank stated that the Talking Page Second Stage Reading Programme would increase the children's reading age by one year per term for an average seven year old, those of the teachers and educationists are frequently less specific and often multiple, e.g. machines may be introduced to give children something to do when the teacher cannot attend to them. For certain audio-visual aids such as tape recorders, the objectives of introducing the equipment to the classroom may be vague or general such as encouraging reading development. However, the research must have a specific framework in order that the comments collected bear some relationship to each other and are of use regarding future decisions concerning the equipment. It is also important in research in schools that the establishment of a framework for the research does not exclude important aspects of the evaluation and that the possibility of effects not originally anticipated will not be overlooked by an overrigid research design; for example, it was suggested that the SRA equipment

might increase the children's independence as well as their reading level and this therefore needed to be considered.

The establishment of objectives may involve a decision on the part of the research worker as to which objectives should be considered the most important and which should therefore be those on which the research is based. Particular care needs to be taken to ensure that the criteria adopted are those which are applicable to the requirements of the evaluation and not just those measurable within the limits of existing technology.

*Evaluation of the machines or the programmes*
In the case of audio-visual aids the definition of objectives is further complicated by the fact that the machine may be considered to have potential apart from the programmes. This problem is of major importance when the machine is not provided with programmes but the teacher has to produce the materials herself. Objectives for such studies therefore should include an assessment of the difficulties faced by teachers in writing programmes as well as an assessment of the effects of programmes. Machines which are supplied with programmes produced by the manufacturer can be seen as a 'package' of programme and machine, one being useless without the other (e.g. the Talking Page) although it could be argued that the potential of the machine needs to be considered, as in the event of the programmes being found faulty but the machine potentially useful, pressure could be brought to bear on the manufacturers to produce alternative programmes.

*Deciding when to evaluate a piece of equipment*
The study of equipment in schools which have not previously used it may produce a novelty effect which boosts the results, or alternatively the teachers' inexperience with the equipment may depress the results. However, if schools are selected which have introduced the equipment prior to the experiment, then such schools may have a high proportion of teachers interested in new techniques who may not be representative of all teachers. Research over a long period may help to provide a measure of this effect but there may be financial limitations on the length of the project. Asking schools to volunteer to take part in the project may ensure that the teachers are interested enough to familiarize themselves with the equipment but again such schools may not be fully representative of all schools as the teachers may introduce an 'enthusiasm' effect on the results. In the London studies schools were selected and then asked if they would like to participate which would be similar to a nonexperimental situation when all schools would be able to decide themselves whether or not to introduce equipment. In the later studies an attempt was made to minimize the novelty effect of the experiment

by allowing the teachers but not the experimental children to use the equipment one term in advance of the study.

*The research design*

Sample selection
A sampling frame has first to be decided on, for example pupils or schools. A sampling frame of pupils is impossible in an audio-visual aids study as aids have to be introduced to whole classes. Therefore schools or classes will form the frame. Sampling can then be totally random which may produce bias due to the large number of variables that exist or the schools may first be stratified on the basis of selected variables, e.g. proportion of immigrants, pupil and teacher turnover, and a number of schools randomly selected from each stratum. Alternatively area sampling can take place to ease the organizational problems of a study, the area being selected as a first stage and the schools from within that area as a second.

The amount of money available determines the size of the project. A decision has to be taken as to whether the equipment purchased should be placed in several classes in a few schools, in which case the operational problems of the study are reduced, or in a few classes in several schools in which case the sensitivity of the experiment in terms of schools representation may be increased. A limited budget may determine that the study is restricted to a small area in order to achieve as representative a sample as possible in one area.

Finally in a study involving audio-visual aids it is important that the schools taking part are willing to cooperate for the period of the project. This was the case for the ILEA studies and therefore the inspectors were asked to recommend cooperative schools from a list of possible schools drawn up by stratified sampling. This of necessity introduces bias into the study, but this bias is necessary if the study is to continue for the required time period.

The multitude of variables involved and the establishment of controls
A major problem in the evaluation of any curriculum innovation is the multitude of variables involved: the child, the school, the teacher, the classroom techniques being used and the innovation. Many of these variables are in themselves multidimensional. Control of some of these variables may not be possible and control of others may not be desirable if the aim is to reproduce the school situation.

Variables relating to the school, e.g. the school's attitude towards different methods of teaching reading, the social and ethnic composition of the school, can be controlled by setting up control and experimental classes within the same school. This, however, is not possible in some schools because of size or organization (e.g. the classes are streamed).

It also does not control for variables such as the quality or attitudes of the individual teacher. Controls can also be set up between schools—one school has all experimental classes and another has all control classes. In both systems of control the Hawthorne effect is likely to operate to some extent, that is the classes (or teachers) will be more affected by participation in the experiment than by the use of the experimental materials. It is possible that the Hawthorne effect will be greater on the control group within the schools where the materials are being used but that in such cases the effect will be more equal to that of the experimental classes. The inclusion of both types of control may provide some measure of whether the Hawthorne effect is working differently in each situation. In addition to the Hawthorne effect, there may be a competitive effect operating in which case the teacher not using the equipment is determined to show that she can produce as good results as the one using the equipment. This will obviously operate in situations where the control class is in the same school as the experimental class.

However in the study of the SRA Reading Laboratories controls were set up both within the experimental schools and in other schools but no differences were found in the results of the two types of control class. Alternatively the same teacher could teach both groups of children but this is not always possible and also does not equalize the children's learning experience as the teacher's attitude to each method may not be the same.

Another system of control is control by analysis of results. The multitude of variables makes the comparison of schools and classes of questionable validity. Comparison between schools is between schools which are not really the same; comparisons between classes within the same school are between teachers who are not the same and between learning situations which have been contaminated by competition. The establishment of the research situation may need to be in terms of one or a mixture of the above situations but the results need not be analysed in terms either of individual classes or schools. Instead, all control classes and all experimental classes can be combined for the analysis and if the numbers taking part in the study are sufficiently large and the selection of schools has been adequately carried out, each group will contain children taught by more experienced and less experienced teachers, more and less competent teachers, teachers with more favourable and less favourable attitudes, in 'traditional' and 'progressive' classes and from different sizes of school and types of school organization. The total control and experimental groups can then be split up in terms of the characteristics of the children and the various subgroups compared, for example children from nonmanual homes using the innovation will be compared with children from nonmanual homes not using the innovation and also with manual children using the innovation; West Indian control children will be compared with West Indian experimental children.

By this method it is possible to establish whether any particular group of children benefits from a particular system to a greater or lesser extent than any other group of children. This is important whatever the research design adopted, as it cannot be assumed that all children react in the same way to a particular learning situation and it is therefore important to establish whether different systems should be adopted with particular groups of children.

The fact that there are a large number of variables involved in a study does not negate the value of that study. If the children who use the aid being studied achieve higher academic standards on average than those not using the technique, despite the variability of teaching received by the total experimental group, then it can be argued that the equipment being studied is itself an effective aid in producing these results. If, however, the results of the control and experimental groups are similar, although within each group there is a considerable variety of results, then it can be argued that it is not the item of equipment that is important in producing these results but some other factor related to the child's learning situation. Research taking place in the field situation has the disadvantage that all the variables cannot be rigidly controlled but it has the advantage that the field situation is closely comparable to the true school situation.

Testing
The need to test children produces problems in the selection of tests. The researcher must decide both the particular skills he wishes to measure, e.g. literacy can mean the ability to decode words, the ability to read and understand a passage or the ability to provide a missing word in a sentence; and with regard to the disruption of classroom routine, what is the minimum number of tests which will produce the required information? He must then decide who should give the tests. Should they be given by external testers or by the teacher? This may depend on the size of the sample which will also determine whether it is feasible to give individual tests or whether group tests should be given. The frequency of testing is also an important problem. Continuous assessment may be desirable in some projects, e.g. in developmental projects such as those of language development, but too frequent testing may in itself affect the results. These factors all have to be considered within the limits of available tests.

Subjective evaluation and monitoring the experiment
Subjective evaluation in the form of the teachers' attitudes to the materials is important in studies of aids to the teaching of reading. The collection of such attitudes involves decisions regarding whether the interview or questionnaire technique is more suitable and how to ensure that the collection of attitudes does not in itself create attitudes.

This is also connected with the probem of monitoring the experiment which is needed to ensure that the teacher using the equipment does so in the specified way for the period of the project. However, too frequent contact with the teacher either for interviewing or for monitoring the experiment may in itself produce a stimulation to good results. A balance therefore has to be maintained between ensuring the materials are correctly used and not contaminating the project. Training in the techniques is also essential. This training may go beyond that which would normally be given if the teachers were not taking part in an experiment, but this may be justified to ensure that the teacher has full knowledge of the aids and can use them correctly.

*Conclusion*

The evaluation of an audio-visual aid or any form of curriculum innovation should not be seen in terms of looking for the one solution to the whole problem of reading. Although it is the inexpensive panacea which is frequently desired when a new aid is introduced to schools, the problem faced by schools in the area of reading is many sided. Schools contain a heterogeneous population for whom different methods of teaching or different teaching aids may have varying degrees of success. It should be the aim of any study to find out for which children and in what specific skills a teaching aid is most effective.

Studies may also need to be designed in such a way that small gains can be recorded. The error limits of many tests may allow for the measurement of fairly large gains, but it may be unrealistic to look for educational innovations which produce either large gains or gains in a short period of time. Mobile populations and lack of resources frequently render impossible research which takes place over a long period. If small gains are measured then the evaluation of the importance of these gains can be made in terms of a cost-benefit analysis. In a situation of scarce resources what magnitude of gain justifies what cost?

The researcher should also be aware of unexpected 'spillover' effects of the innovation and possibly follow them up at a later stage; for example, it was suggested by one secondary school teacher taking part in the study of the SRA Reading Laboratories that the introduction of the laboratories had aroused the interest of her students to such an extent that she had higher attendance rates on a Friday afternoon (one of the occasions when the laboratory was used) than she had ever had previously. The limitations of the study should also be borne in mind (its size, measuring techniques used etc) in the presentation of results so that a balanced view is given in the report. The reader must have sufficient information to judge the relevance of the criteria used and the techniques by which they have been measured.

In conclusion the problems discussed here have been particularly related to research in the 'real-life' school situation. Many but not all are common to other types of evaluation. The style of research selected should not be related primarily to the problems likely to be encountered but should be the most appropriate to the questions which it is hoped the evaluation will answer.

# Part three The development of reading skills

## 4 Towards a theory of literacy

*Jessie F. Reid*

It seems important to begin this paper with some discussion of the meaning to be attached in it to the term 'theory'. The reason is that the term theory is for many people a loaded one, and there is a long-standing antithesis, in the history of many disciplines, between theory on the one hand and practice on the other. Moreover, this antithesis has tended to be to the detriment of attempts at theoretical study because it has often been made in the context of an assertion that something or other 'is all right in theory but does not work in practice'. Indeed feelings often exist that the person who is in touch with what goes on in the field is at a distinct advantage when it comes to knowing what to do, compared with the 'theorist' who sits in some remote ivory tower and just thinks about the problem. Theory may sometimes be seen then as something remote and irrelevant. I would submit that this view is quite mistaken.

Descriptive or explanatory theory in any given area of study consists in some systematic and coherent account of how things are: for instance, of how phenomena are to be classified; of how growth and development proceed; of how apparently disparate phenomena can be reconciled. (It is of course also possible in certain fields to develop *prescriptive* theory—that is, theory about what it is desirable to aim at; but in this present context aims are not the main issue.) Among the important characteristics of descriptive or explanatory theory, one of the most vital to the present argument is that it is—and indeed must be—rooted in observation. It does not of course remain at the level of observation: it is also essentially the result of the operation of the human intellect and the human imagination upon observations—trying to reduce them to order and system, trying to find explanatory rules and test these by prediction and, perhaps most important of all, trying always to integrate more and more of what is observed into the coherent conceptual system that is being built.

The criticism that a particular recommended course of action, based on theory, 'does not work' amounts to an assertion that the action does not produce some predicted effect. This may well be because the theory from which the recommendations for application are derived is in some way inadequate; or it may be because the problems of applying theory to particular situations have not been properly solved. But in either case, there is no reason to conclude that we can do without theory. On the contrary, the conclusion must be that renewed efforts at the development and application of theory are called for.

There is in existence an enormous literature on how to teach reading and writing. There is also a very large body of experimental study, much of it conducted in a laboratory rather than a classroom setting, and concerned often with very small and restricted segments of reading behaviour. Isolating and studying small segments is of course one of the classical methods of trying to advance detailed understanding, but it brings in its train the tremendous difficulty of trying to keep track of and synthesize the results. The fact that there have been relatively few attempts to produce a coherent and unified account of what goes on when a child is learning to become literate, and of what goes on in the performance of the skilled, mature reader and writer, cannot however be attributed entirely to communication difficulties. In the manual to *Breakthrough to Literacy,* Mackay, Thompson and Schaub (1970) put forward the view that the absence of a coherent theory of literacy is due to the long domination of the field of literacy studies by experimental psychology. It is undoubtedly true that books on the teaching of reading such as *The Improvement of Reading* (Gates 1935) or *The Psychology of Teaching Reading* (Anderson and Dearborn 1952) drew heavily on the results of studies of a psychological type—studies of perception, of discrimination, of eye movements, of memorizing, of vocabulary and so on. The point made by Mackay *et al* is that books like these failed to take adequate account of reading and writing as kinds of language learning and as kinds of learning which took place in a particular social and cultural context.

If one looks at the literature on reading which has appeared during the last ten or fifteen years, there is no doubt that the shift to an emphasis on reading as language learning rather than reading as perceptual learning is the feature of major and outstanding importance. In this same span of time, language learning itself has been set in a new context, partly through the rise of psycholinguistics and partly through the work of sociologists interested in the effects of subcultures on language development and language use. It is true, too, that people interested in the learning of literacy have been developing an interest in linguistics and psycholinguistics, while linguists, psycholinguists and experimental psychologists have been developing an interest in the learning of reading and writing as important manifestations of language learning. The breakdown of barriers which Mackay *et al* consider so important has therefore already been happening.

Perhaps the time has come when one can try to indicate some general

C

lines along which the building of a theory of literacy might now proceed further—a theory which makes use of the most significant findings at present available from psychology, from linguistics and psycholinguistics, and from sociology.

It is a long time since the observation was made that the perception of words is a rather special case of form perception. Before the beginning of this century Cattell had conducted experiments which showed that under tachistoscopic presentation single words were recognized as quickly as single letters and that either sentences were grasped completely or else few, if any, of the individual words or letters were read. These observations were commented on by Huey (1908) in his now famous but long neglected book *The Psychology and Pedagogy of Reading*; but perhaps because of the tendency at the time to see the results in terms of Gestalt psychology rather than in terms of a theory of language learning, not a great deal of use seems to have been made, in subsequent research on the relationship of visual perception to the learning of reading, of Cattell's very significant findings. It is interesting, for instance, that some tests of 'visual perception' which have been used to study the abilities of children in this area have included material which not only does not consist of words or letters but involves shapes which are not even, to use the term made familiar by Gibson *et al* (1962a), 'letter-like'. Yet there is evidence from several studies that training in general visual form perception does not necessarily transfer to the reading task, (see Weintraub 1968 for a review of this literature). On the other hand, Gibson's famous study of letter-like forms and some recent studies of the perception of printed material seem to be yielding more promising results. These are studies of subjects who are at some stage in the process of learning to become mature readers, and they are studies which take account of the fact that what is being perceived is material which is capable of being linguistically organized at some level. For instance, the work of Gibson *et al* (1962, 1963) on the relation of grapheme perception to pronounceability, work which has an obvious affinity with the early work of Cattell to which I have referred, shows that adults use their implicit knowledge of phonological constraints in their native language to aid them in the retention and recognition of letter groups and that this ability can be seen developing in children between the ages of seven and nine. It has also been shown by Epstein (1961) that retention of words which are syntactically structured (even though the sentence is meaningless) is higher than that for the same words in a random order. Morton (1964) showed how speed, accuracy and eye-voice span were affected in mature adult readers by the degree of approximation to English of word strings; and Merritt (1968) showed how the speed and accuracy with which children read strings of simple words was similarly affected by the degree of approximation to English. Schlesinger (1969) reports experimental work which shows that the syntactic structure of prose is significantly related to the way in which the adult reader can scan the prose in 'chunks'.

I have used these references as an introductory illustration of the main theme of this discussion. All of them are in a sense studies of the visual perception of printed material; but the important thing about them is that they are studies of the integration by the subject of visual perceptual skill and other skills—in the cases I have quoted, linguistic skills of various kinds. The view which I want to put forward here is that one way of advance towards a coherent theory of literacy now appears to be in the detailed study of integrative activity on the part of readers, whether they are learners, or subjects who have already acquired a high level of proficiency. In other words I am suggesting that the synthesis of which I spoke earlier cannot be done by the individual research worker who simply looks at the studies in separate areas and then tries to put the results together in his head, nor even by groups of specialists in conference. What we must also do is look at how the reader fuses his skills together in action.

This approach has come to seem especially appropriate because it is now becoming clear that even the early learning of reading is a process in which the learner has to do a great many things at the same time. All methods for teaching children to read have embodied some notion of simplification. Long ago it was perhaps more plausible than it is now to think of the child at the very beginning as doing his learning in only one area—that is he was learning, a hundred years ago, to associate single letters with single sounds or to associate letter shapes with their names and then learning how simple written words were spelt. But if we think about even this logically simplified learning, we realize that it presupposes that the child has understood something of what is meant by speech sounds, and it also presupposes that he is able to perceive and learn sequences in a horizontal plane. Nowadays, however, children are not taught to read in this way. Simplification now takes a different form—that of giving them content which will be relevant and one hopes interesting, a vocabulary within their comprehension, contexts for the use of the written word which make sense to them and, increasingly, syntactic structures which follow the patterns they use in their speech. But this change has almost destroyed the distinction which used to be made between the mechanics of reading and reading comprehension. Moreover, it has brought into much greater prominence at an early stage those skills which make use of the oral language competence which a child already possesses. And it means that the learner is now, more than ever, having to develop and use from the beginning what may be called 'integrating skills', cognitive skills which enable him to fuse information from different sources.

One might well ask at this point why it is necessary to introduce the concept of such a set of skills at all. Certainly, a theory should above all be economical, and not multiply hypotheses beyond what is necessary. But there are several indications in recent work that some such concept is necessary if we are to make sense of the evidence.

The concept has already been introduced in several contexts, some-times—though not always—by people concerned with reading failure. Work on auditory-visual integration and cross-modal transfer has been reviewed recently by Cashdan (1969). In his discussion, he suggests that there is a gap in our understanding of the 'totality of reading ability', and draws attention to the little-understood role of verbal mediation. In a recent exposition of the role of 'intermediate skills' Merritt (1969) emphasizes the importance of the ability to 'respond simultaneously to a variety of kinds of sequence', and goes on to emphasize the need for more specific teaching, including discussion with children of what makes a text 'readable' at a given level of competence. Johnson and Myklebust (1967), discussing reading failure, believe that integrative activity is crucial and that much reading breakdown takes place at this level. They suggest, however, that there are different kinds of linkage between modalities and systems, and that true 'integrative learning' is where all the systems (visual, auditory, tactile and kinaesthetic) function as a unit.

The group of studies I began by discussing can be seen as illustrating the functioning of various types of learned integration within the field of written language but below the level of sentence meaning. A further relevant area of recent study has been concerned with children's errors in reading aloud. The four to which I want to refer here are by Good-man (1967), Clay (1969), Weber (1970) and Beimiller (1970). These studies have two features in common. One is a concentration on the degree to which children's use of their oral language competence is reflected in the errors in their early reading. The second is an interest in some aspect of learning which involves the bringing together of different reading skills. All four studies show that the greater proportion of errors in the reading of children in their first year are syntactically correct—that is to say, they consist of an acceptable part of speech in terms of the preceding words in the sentence. Goodman notes also children's tendency to rearrange language forms in their reading books to conform more closely to the syntax of speech, and affirms that even early read-ing is not mere sequential processing, but (to quote his title) 'a psycho-linguistic guessing game'. Clay studied not only errors but self-correction behaviour, and noticed how children progressed to a closer and closer match between what they thought should be, and what actually was on the page. This closer approximation appeared both at a word level and at the level of matching the number of syllables in a phrase to the number of syllables uttered. In her discussion, Clay draws on the notion of 'parallel processing' developed by Niesser (1966). Weber, in a somewhat similar study of errors, showed that the instances of correct syntactic matching of errors to the syntax of the part of the sentence which followed were much less frequent than matching to the syntax of the part which preceded, but that as many as two thirds of the errors were acceptable to both preceding and following parts. She notes what she describes as a progressive 'refinement of strategies' in the use of various sources of information, and a developing ability to take account of increasingly large units of preceding context. Beimiller found what he took to be three stages in the process of integrating knowledge of spelling rules with awareness of the syntax and the meaning. He identified an early period of 'response errors' which again showed the high proportion of syntactical agreement found by Clay and Weber. His second stage, which he called the period of 'nonresponse errors', was followed by a third stage where the children again offered a response but this time one which was much more in agreement with the visual information, that is with the spelling pattern. He concludes that the intervening period, in which there was an increasing tendency to nonresponse errors, represented a stage when the child was attempting to take account of at least two kinds of information at once, and was therefore having to begin to use what I am calling an integrating skill.

I referred to at least two kinds of information because so far I have not discussed the complexity of what we refer to as 'context'. The studies by Clay and Weber showed that the proportion of errors which were syntactically correct—that is, which were an acceptable part of speech in terms of the syntax—was greater than the proportion which was also semantically correct—that is, which made sense in terms of what the sentence, or the paragraph, was about. These studies draw attention, then, to the fact that there are at least three components of context with which quite young children have to deal and these are not always coincidental. So here again we find the necessity for another integrating skill—the integrating this time of the implicit sense of the syntax with the 'meaning', with what the sentence is about, with what the preceding sentence was about, with the way the story or the episode, the general sequence in the written text, is moving. Memory, comprehension and anticipation are all involved. If we try to enhance or clarify context by providing illustrations, we give the child yet another integrating task: this time a task of interpreting some material which is not in the form of words and using his interpretation of this in a way which illuminates his interpretation of the text. So that while in one sense illustrations may be a help, they call for some kind of cognitive activity which would not be called for if they were not there.

There is of course an important relationship between this early, primitive prediction from syntactic and semantic context and the fluent anticipatory process which Merritt (1969) describes in his discussion of 'intermediate skills'. The young children in the four studies mentioned above were using prediction in many cases as a substitute for word-decoding, or word-recognition, in situations where their knowledge was inadequate. The developed intermediate skills enable a reader to use prediction to narrow the field of possibilities, to render certain elements in a visual array redundant, to reduce the decoding load. When they are effectively present, integration has already taken place.

The existence of those areas of integration and the fact that the skills called for are, at least in part, cognitive, makes it reasonable to look at the language which is used to talk about the learning involved. Reid (1966) and Downing (1970) showed that some children of five who were in the early stages of learning to read had great difficulty in thinking and talking about what they were doing, partly because they did not have a vocabulary which helped them to do it. For instance, they tended to refer to letters as 'numbers', and later moved on, when the distinction between numbers and letters had become clear to them, to referring to letters as 'words', which of course merely introduced another confusion. They tended to confuse 'sounding' and 'spelling'. They did not know the word 'sentence' and commonly referred to sentence as 'stories', which left them with no term for an extended episode or narrative. They referred also to words as 'names' and some of them seemed to make a distinction between written words which were 'words' and those which were 'not words'. In short, they were seen to be in a state of considerable conceptual confusion which was in part a reflection of the teachers' attempts to avoid all reference to what might be called the technical terminology of literacy. While conducting my evaluation of *Breakthrough to Literacy* (Reid, in press) I was able to observe the effect on children of the same age and ability range of having these terms—letter, word, sentence, and so on—used freely in discussion. I found a marked improvement in the children's ability to use the terms and to make many of the conceptual distinctions for which these stand. This seemed clearly to be the outcome of the deliberate use of the terms by teachers, in teaching situations which lent themselves to free discussion of the writing system. The task of learning and using the terminology, then, is not beyond the powers of the five or six year old. We do not yet know, however, what its exact role may be in the acquisition of literacy; but we cannot ignore the possibility that it may be crucial for some children not only in the initial stages, but also at those later stages when they have to make the transition to the registers of written language found in their extension readers, in their textbooks, and in all the resource material which modern approaches to the language arts require them to use.

It seems to me therefore that one important next step in theory building is to extend the study of areas of integration and to combine this with a study of the particular cognitive skills and of the language relevant to them. And I think this means that we need, in addition to the controlled and structured research with which we are familiar, more studies of children learning and of teachers teaching, using techniques of classroom observation.

It may well be that a great deal of the hold-up with poorer readers resides not just in such tasks as the integration of stimuli in different sensory modalities, but in their inability to perform such cognitive acts as suspending judgment until more information is processed; modifying a first guess (or 'hypothesis') in the light of further information; transferring information from the short-term to medium-term memory (Graham 1970); or fusing information from different cognitive systems. Study of the way in which the dialogue between learner and teacher can contribute to the strengthening of these cognitive skills may have much to offer both to the theorists and to the practitioners in whose ultimate interest they work.

*References*

ANDERSON, I. H. and DEARBORN, W. F. (1952) *The Psychology of Teaching Reading* New York: Ronald Press Company

BEIMILLER, A. (1970) The development of the use of graphic and contextual information as children learn to read *Reading Research Quarterly* 6, 1, 75–96

CASHDAN, A. (1969) 'Backward readers—research on auditory-visual integration' in K. Gardner (ed) *Reading Skills: Theory and Practice* London: Ward Lock Educational

CLAY, MARIE (1969) Reading errors and self-correction behaviour *British Journal of Educational Psychology* 39, 1, 47–56

DOWNING, J. (1970) Children's concepts of language in learning to read *Educational Research* 12, 2, 106–112

EPSTEIN, W. (1961) The influence of syntactic structure on learning *American Journal of Psychology* 74, 80–85

GATES, ARTHUR (1935) *The Improvement of Reading* New York: Macmillan

GIBSON, E. J., GIBSON, J. J., DAVIDSON, A. and OSSER, H. (1962a) A developmental study of the discrimination of letter-like forms *Journal of Comparative and Physiological Psychology* 55, 897–906

GIBSON, E. J., PICK, A. D., OSSER, H. and HAMMOND, M. (1962) The role of grapheme-phoneme correspondence in the perception of words *American Journal of Psychology* 75, 554–570

GIBSON, E. J., OSSER, H. and PICK, A. D. (1963) A study of the development of grapheme-phoneme correspondence *Journal of Verbal Learning and Verbal Behaviour* 2, 142–146

GOODMAN, K. (1967) *Reading: A Psycholinguistic Guessing Game* Address to the American Educational Research Association New York, February 16th

GRAHAM, NORMAN (1970) *The Language of Educationally Subnormal Children* Birmingham: School of Education, University of Birmingham

HUEY, E. B. (1908) *The Psychology and Pedagogy of Reading* New York: Macmillan (republished 1969 by MIT Press)

JOHNSON, D. and MYKLEBUST, H. (1967) *Learning Disabilities: Educational Principles and Practices* New York: Grune and Stratton

MACKAY, D., THOMPSON, B., and SCHAUB, P. (1970) *Breakthrough to Literacy* London: Longman

MERRITT, J. E. (1968) Assessment of reading ability: a new range of diagnostic tests? *Reading*, 2, 2, 8–16

MERRITT, J. E. (1969) 'The intermediate skills' in K. Gardner (ed) *Reading Skills: Theory and Practice* London: Ward Lock Educational

MORTON, J. (1964) The effects of context upon speed of reading, eye movements and eye-voice span *Quarterly Journal of Experimental Psychology* 16, 340–355

NEISSER, U. (1966) *Cognitive Psychology* New York: Appleton-Century-Crofts

REID, J. F. (1966) Learning to think about reading *Educational Research* 9, 1, 56–62

REID, J. F. (in press) *Breakthrough in Action* London: Longman

SCHLESINGER, I. M. (1969) *Sentence Structure and the Reading Process* The Hague: Mouton

WEBER, ROSE-MARIE (1970) A linguistic analysis of first-grade reading errors *Reading Research Quarterly* 5, 3

WEINTRAUB, S. (1968) 'Visual perceptual factors in reading' in M. Clark and S. Maxwell (eds) *Reading: Influences on Progress* Proceedings Fifth Annual Study Conference UKRA, Edinburgh

# 5 Readiness for school: a look at some critical issues

*Gilbert R. Gredler*

It is my contention that the topic of 'readiness' for first grade is more complicated because many of the 'right' questions have not been asked in the first place. Many studies, for example, do show that 'underage' children do less well than older children in first grade and subsequent grades of school. We need to ask, however, whether this is an adequate criterion. Should younger children have to meet the criterion of success which is defined by what the older children have accomplished? What would be an adequate criterion of success for children of younger age? Thus we need to look at the underlying assumptions of the research projects.

Some of the questions to be considered are:

1 Why do most school personnel in the United States seek to delay a child's entrance into school?
2 Why is there an emphasis on the negative factors: damage to vision, emotional problems etc?
3 Why do school personnel constantly talk about children 'not making it' and not seek out children who obviously are quite 'ready' and may be even able to go into second grade after a few weeks?

It is the writer's contention that none of these questions are answered by looking only at the research evidence on the first grade children. It is only by looking at the issue from a broad social science background that at least some of the right questions may be asked and some light cast on why the area of readiness has become so important as an area of debate.

*Legitimate questions to ask about entrance age to school*
There are many legitimate questions to be asked concerning the beginning date of school for children. Among such questions are the following:

1 What is the role of 'maturation' in the readiness of the child for school? This is a central issue in the field of child development. For example, if we hold to an educational philosophy that says we should allow a five year old to read and we make an attempt to teach him,

do the 'facts' in the field of child development say this can be done?

2  What is the role of teaching methodology in this whole question? Is it possible that if a different teaching method were used in a school system there would be an increase in the number of 'younger' children who could learn to read adequately?

3  What criteria should be used to ascertain if children of varying chronological ages are actually successful in learning how to read? Is an absolute criterion of a certain grade placement score to be reached by the end of the year adequate?

4  What is the role of organizational forces in relation to this whole issue? What factors exist within the organization of the school system which make for emphasis on finding *the right age* for beginning school?

*Organizational and sociological theory as applied to the school*
A frame of reference is needed to look at the host of questions raised thus far.

In the phraseology of Carlson (1964), the school can be called a 'domesticated organization' meaning it is an organization that does not compete with other organizations for 'clients'; in fact, just the opposite occurs—there is a continual stream of individuals always available and ready to enter the institution. Carlson points out that this kind of organization does not have to struggle for survival and that its existence is guaranteed.

In Carlson's view, such organizations are, because of their protected status, slower to change and adapt to the changing society which they serve. He also states that when an organization exists that cannot control the entrance of its clients, it makes special arrangements to adapt to this flow of clients. Carlson hypothesizes that such an organization has certain goals (in the case of the school, graduating a person who knows how to read, do maths etc) which they hold as worthwhile objectives and which cannot be realized adequately through the presence of un-selected clients. Personnel running such an organization will look constantly for ways and means of reducing the disruptive effect of having completely unselected clients. Thus it is possible that one of the reasons for the extreme emphasis by teachers on the entrance age factor and their insistence on raising it is an attempt to cut down the size and scope of the unselected clientele.

It is obviously easier to attempt the line of attack described above rather than make continual adjustment within the organization itself. Carlson points out that one adaptive response of domesticated organizations to unselected clients is segregation. In regard to primary grade children in America, this is increasingly taking the form of transition classes from kindergarten to first grade in addition to the usual special education classes. However, no matter what the entrance age is in a school system, there always appear to be children who still aren't ready for first grade. While the author feels that a transition class has definite potential in helping children improve their performance, in actual fact the usual transition class is a dumping ground where the child 'repeats' kindergarten. Here he stays another year without having the epithet hurled that he has 'failed' kindergarten. In addition, existence of such a class relieves the anxiety of school personnel in regard to the children who are failing.

It is obvious that education personnel are concerned about the success of the students moving through the organization. As we have said, the resultant anxiety is frequently reflected into overconcern about the child's chronological age and maturity at the time of entrance to school. Obviously we now have a point of conflict here between the needs of the personnel in the organization (i.e. school) and the parents of the child beginning school.

Our main question here is how can an organization which has to deal with unselected clients deal with them in a legitimate way? Is there any way the organization could attempt to cope with the problem other than by exclusion? When the present organizational structure has as its main way of dealing with 'individual differences' the self-contained classroom with thirty children and one teacher, then we can be certain the organization will have difficulty meeting all the individual needs of its children. Under such conditions emphasis will continually be on selecting out in one way or another the individuals who will not 'make' it. The teacher will continually be upset about the children who are 'immature', who are not yet six years of age, boys etc—all groups which the agents of the organization are *sure* are extreme risks for first grade work.

The emphasis on increase in entrance age is also due in part to the fact that the teacher's responsibility goes beyond the authority allotted to her. Anderson (1967) points out that the teacher does not have the authority to control many variables which will affect the progress of her class (i.e. low ability students, discipline problems, emotional maladjustment) yet she has some responsibility for showing progress with each.

Frequently, the teacher will also lack the requisite background of specialized knowledge to deal with many of the problems before her. In such a situation Anderson maintains that the personnel in the organization (teachers and auxiliary personnel) will minimize their responsibility to act in such cases and will attempt to shift responsibility elsewhere. Thus we have the development by the teacher of ways of getting rid of the problems that are difficult.

There are continual attempts to define and redefine normality in the light of the school personnel's desire to get rid of problems rather than work with children who have problems. The current group with which one is working often defines normality. For example, if a sixth grade class contains pupils in which the majority read between the fifth and seventh grade level, then a child at the third grade level will be seen as deviant, as having a serious reading problem (Lauer). However, if this particular child is found in a classroom group where the average reading level is at the second grade, then this pupil is often not considered to be deviant at all in his reading performance. Lauer mentions how the search goes on constantly to remove from the group individuals at the tail end of the distribution. However, no matter how many special classes or groupings there are within the system, the search seems to continue and more and more people are separated out from the normal group.

The same situation holds for the entrance age variable. The hue and cry continues for a higher entrance age so that fewer children will come to school who are 'not ready'. No matter what the entrance age — September 1st or December 1st — teachers complain that there is a group which is 'too young'. Teachers in school system Y (an upper middle class system) where the entrance age is high (six years by September 1st) complain regularly of a group 'too young' to profit from school while teachers in school system Z where the entrance age limit is December 30th, also complain regularly of a group 'too young'.

*Readiness versus maturation*
It is obvious that many individuals are confusing readiness with maturation. Washburne (1936), puts it thus: '(There are many factors which) must be taken into account if we are not to force open a bud not yet ready to bloom.'

The emphasis on maturation as *the* avenue of readiness led to emphasis in the schools on postponement of various subjects until the child showed adequate readiness. However as Tyler (1964) points out, even at the time that the unfolding concept of readiness was being promulgated, other educators such as Brownell (1938) and Buswell (1938) were arguing that such an approach to readiness took into account only the kinds of methods and material currently in use. In discussing the age to begin reading instruction, Gates (1937) put the issue quite well. He said that it is not merely a question of determining the success of pupils at different times; to do this 'may merely tell us how difficult the materials and methods are rather than when, all things, especially social and educational values, being considered, it is best for a child to learn to read'.

The validity of this point is illustrated by the important study done by Gates over thirty years ago. In comparing four groups of first grade children, Gates found the minimum mental age necessary as a requisite for a successful first grade experience differed among the four groups studied. Gates relates the difference in mental age to the differences in methods employed by the teachers involved. However, the maturation 'school' was in ascendency in American education and at the time this study was reported, little attention was paid to Gates's results.

The maturational school of thought has been championed in the United States by Hymes (1958) and Gesell (1954) and subsequently today by Ames (1967). In *Is Your Child in the Wrong Grade?* Ames (1967) popularizes the maturational approach to the extent that she suggests that up to two thirds of all school children are overplaced in school.

In some education circles, emphasis on the developmental stages of Gesell *et al* as the sine qua non of determiners of school readiness has given way to emphasis on Piaget's stages of intellectual development.

*Studies of entrance age*
When statistically significant differences in achievement are found between older and younger children, can we then draw the conclusion that the younger pupils have performed inadequately? If we accept this conclusion as valid, we are saying that the older child will be more successful than the younger child. But success is being defined by what the older child does do and what the younger child should be doing. In view of the difference chronologically, it is fallacious reasoning to expect the same level of performance from the younger child.

Green (1962) makes an important point when he states that older pupils can be said to have learned more in school only if the assumption is made that the older group did not know more than the younger group when they began school. He goes on to say that this assumption is false, since scores on readiness tests show a positive relationship to the child's age. What needs to be emphasized is that the school in its evaluation practices should not use such practices which automatically put the younger group at a disadvantage. It appears obvious that teachers are using some variant of the normal distribution curve in assigning marks. With older children coming into school with up to an additional year of experience accruing from their extra year of chronological age and scoring higher on achievement tests, the younger children are thus relegated to a lower position in a total ranking of students.

Few of the studies done in the area of entrance age even consider the adequacy of the achievement level that has been attained by the younger entrants. Despite the differences that do obtain between younger and older children on standardized tests or grades, shouldn't we also ask if the achievement level of the younger entrants reached a *satisfactory* level?

It is obvious that if educators wished to find highly significant differences between groups of children, they would turn to socioeconomic groupings rather than stressing sex differences. Anyone looking at data on readiness levels or achievement levels of first grade children from culturally deprived groups versus middle class groups cannot fail to be impressed with the enormity of the gap usually found. For example, data from Kellmer Pringle *et al* (1966) on seven year olds show that differences based on socioeconomic status show a range of 32.3 per cent between those who are good readers in socioeconomic group I (professional status) versus socioeconomic group V (labourers).

While it has been frequently proposed in comparisons of underage or overage children that the underage wait a year or the date of entrance be changed upward, no educator has recently called for a delay in entrance to school based on the differences in readiness among the various socioeconomic classes.

*Studies from European countries*
In studying factors involved in readiness for first grade, it is important to look at the contributions of investigators from countries other than the United States.

Of particular interest in Malmquist's (1958) study is the composition of the school population. In Sweden, children do not enter school until they are seven years of age. Since many individuals in the United States believe that the entrance age should be raised, it should be helpful to look at the performance of children who enter at even a later age than in America.

The mean mental age of the group of children studied by Malmquist was eight years four months. Even with this high mental age, 21 per cent of the total school population sampled were still categorized as children with special reading disabilities.

Eye-opening as Malmquist's data are, we need to look at some British research which will also undoubtedly upset many who believe in the value of a higher entrance age. Kellmer Pringle *et al* (1966) investigated several factors in the development of 11,000 seven year olds in Great Britain. It should be noted that children enter infant school (i.e. primary school) in Great Britain usually at the beginning of the term in which they reach the age of five.

Kellmer Pringle's data show quite clearly that a substantial number of children in both the younger and older groups were achieving at an adequate level in reading. It is interesting to note that both groups would be in kindergarten in the United States. In this study the effect of a longer school period evidently overrides their early age at school entrance.

Kellmer Pringle's data also show how influential the socioeconomic variable is in the adjustment of these school children. Over three-quarters of the children from socioeconomic levels I and II are considered 'stable' regardless of the time they entered school or length of time spent in school. However, the percentage of stable children drops drastically when we look at occupational levels IV and V.

*Some American studies*
In the late 1950s, concern was expressed in Ohio about the failure rate in first grade. Consideration was given to changing the entrance age to require a child to be older when he began school. Entrance age was determined by local boards, but generally children were accepted up to December 31st. At that time, the move for a higher entrance age was defeated, but subsequently (1965) the state adopted an entrance age cutoff of October 31st. As of 1969, the state mandated a cutoff of September 30th.

In 1956 failures in the first grades of the Canton, Ohio school system were studied (Gredler 1956). Children could enter first grade if they attained their sixth birthday by December 31st. Pupils were divided into four age groups each of which differed by a three month age range. Children in the January-March range were the oldest and those born in the October-December period were the youngest.

There was a significant difference in failure rate between various age categories. In further analysis of the data, school by school, however, it was discovered that there was a tremendous variability in failure rate.

In this analysis the following data came to light:

1 Four (14 per cent) of the twenty-eight schools in the system contributed one third of all the failures.
2 These four schools were all situated in low socioeconomic sections of the city. Removing failures in these four schools from the data resulted in a nonsignificant relationship between failures and being underage. This is another example of the influence of the socioeconomic variable on achievement.

Six schools contributed 45 per cent of all the failures. These six schools included the above four and two serving upper-lower socioeconomic class. In view of the disproportionate influence of these few schools on the failure rate, the superintendent recommended no change in the entrance age. Here a social criterion instead of a statistical criterion was utilized in making the decision not to change the entrance age.

*Summary of the readiness issue*
1 During the last seventeen years, there has been a consistent trend to raise the entrance age in American schools for children entering first grade.
2 Evidence is continually offered that overage children do better in school than underage children. Many of the studies which show

this difference have failed to take into account the differences which are already in existence between the older and younger pupils when they enter school. Investigators have frequently used as a criterion of first grade success the achievement level reached by the older child. If the younger child does not reach this level, then he is considered as unsuccessful. Such fallacious reasoning has complicated the issue of the entrance age controversy.

3 Analysis of the academic performance of children in foreign school systems indicate that many children can do successful first grade work at a younger age than American children without harm to their physical health. Conversely, the high percentage of underachievers found in school populations composed of children who enter school a year later than in America indicates that a higher entrance age per se is no panacea in reducing the percentage of academic failures.

*References*

AMES, L. B. (1967) *Is Your Child in the Wrong Grade?* New York: Harper and Row

ANDERSON, J. G. (1967) Bureaucratic rule: bearers of organizational authority *Educational Administration* 2

BROWNELL, W. A. (1938) A critique of the committee of seven's investigation on the grade placement of arithmetic topics *The Elementary School Journal* 38, 7, 495–508

BUSWELL, G. T. (1938) Deferred arithmetic *Mathematics Teacher* 31

CARLSON, R. O. (1964) Environmental constraints and organizational consequence: the public school and its clients in *63rd Yearbook National Society for Study of Education* Chicago: University of Chicago Press

GATES, A. I. (1937) The necessary mental age for beginning reading *The Elementary School Journal* 37, 7, 497–508

GESELL, A. (1954) 'The ontogenesis of infant behaviour' in L. Carmichael (ed) *Manual of Child Psychology* New York: John Wiley and Sons

GREDLER, G. R. (1956) A study of first grade failures Unpublished study Ohio: Canton Board of Education

GREEN, D. R. and SIMMONS, S. V. (1962) Chronological age and school entrance *The Elementary School Journal* October, 62, 41–47

HYMES, J. L. (1958) *Before the Child Reads* Evanston, Illinois: Row Peterson

KELLMER PRINGLE, M. L., BUTLER, M. R. and DAVIE, R. (1966) *11,000 Seven Year Olds* London: Longman

LAUER, R. M. (no date) On the concept of normality and deviation: their implications for innovations in the roles of school psychologists Unpublished paper

MALMQUIST, E. (1958) *Factors Related to Reading Disabilities in the*

*First Grade of the Elementary School* Stockholm: Almqvist and Wiksell

TYLER, F. T. (1964) Issues related to readiness to learn in *63rd Yearbook of the National Society for the Study of Education* Chicago: University of Chicago Press

WASHBURNE, C. W. (1936) Ripeness *Progressive Education* 13

D

# 6 The development of beginning reading skills: recent findings

*Madeline I. Hardy*

For more than thirty years a great controversy has continued over how young children should be taught to read. No area of the curriculum has been more thoroughly researched than reading, and according to Smith (1961), the last fifty years have seen more innovations in beginning reading instruction and methods than the previous three hundred. However, many of these new programme and methods have had no strong base in theory, have been conceived on the basis of intuition, and have hence been short-lived.

*'New' research in beginning reading*
Before 1960 most reading research was conducted with adults, and little was known of how children became skilled readers. Moreover, the studies of adult reading were mainly in the area of visual discrimination of letters and words (Levin and Williams 1970). However, since 1960 a notable change in the nature of beginning reading research has taken place. In the early 1960s the United States Office of Education conducted exhaustive surveys of reading in the first two elementary grades. These studies were useful in assessing instructional methods and practices but failed to shed light upon the basic nature of the reading process. Again Chall's work (1967), in which the Carnegie Corporation supported the analysis of the 'great debate' in reading up to 1965, while endorsing a methodology, i.e. the code-breaking as opposed to the meaning approach in beginning reading, failed to answer some fundamental questions.

A number of projects across North America are now searching for answers to the beginning reading dilemma. The major focus of these studies is those aspects of beginning reading which involve decoding or translating from the printed to the spoken form of language. Various disciplines are becoming involved including psychology, linguistics, and psycholinguistics.

*The nature of beginning reading*
Two basic questions concerning beginning reading search for answers: What does beginning reading involve? How does a child learn to read most efficiently? Though apparently simple, these are complex questions. As early as 1908, Huey said: '... to completely analyse what we do when we read would almost be the acme of the psychologists' achieve-

46

ments, for it would be to describe very many of the most intricate workings of the human mind. . . .' According to Betts (1971) '. . . a beginning reader must deal with imperfect symbols for speech by learning to use a complex of processes which are speculated about rather than understood by scientists. . . .'

Although little is known of how young children learn to read, each year millions of them accomplish the task. In fact, if intelligent children who were also neurologically and emotionally intact were motivated to learn to read, provided with materials, and left to their own devices, many of them would learn on their own. For many others, however, such conditions would not produce reading success, nor do seemingly ideal situations lead to achievement in reading for this group of children. If fundamental knowledge about the reading process could be obtained and could become the basis for the development of precise and sequential instructional materials, the implications for beginning reading success could be exciting (Crosby 1969).

As one of the language skills, what is unique about beginning reading? Venezky (1966) considers the decoding aspect (the translation from written symbols to sound) unique, since comprehension is involved in the other language skills of speech and writing, but decoding is not a component of either of these skills. The translation or decoding process is made complex by the very nature of the graphic symbols of the language, which must be differentiated. Letters are of various sizes, printed or written, capital or lower-case, and different type faces are used. Differences in orientation are critical. For young children, a chair is a chair whether it is standing up, lying down, on its side, or under a table, but b can be d, p, or q, depending upon its position.

The nature of the beginning reading process, then, is being extensively investigated, and the results promise to be fruitful.

*The London (Canada) Board of Education Research Project in Elemental Reading Skills*
Impetus for the research in elemental reading skills being conducted in London came from a continuing concern regarding problems in reading and language among students in the school system. The growing numbers of students requiring remedial help in reading, a situation by no means unique to the London school system, led to consideration of preventive solutions. A search for basic developmental data documenting the normal growth of beginning reading abilities was fruitless. Such data have not been developed and there is some question whether they can be developed. Do children learn in a sufficiently orderly fashion to allow generalizations about the developmental pattern of reading skills or are language patterns so individual and unique that this is impossible?

The acquisition of basic developmental data regarding beginning reading is essential as a basis for the creation of tests and curriculum materials. How, for example, do the publishers and authors of reading tests and materials determine the specifications for their publications? How do they decide what concepts should be tested or introduced, and in what order? Apparently simple questions are really very complex. Considering the teaching of the alphabet to young children, questions such as the following arise:

1 In what order should the alphabet letters be taught?
2 Should upper and lower-case be taught at the same time or separately?
3 What activities should be included in teaching the names of the alphabet letters—singing them, repeating them by rote?
4 In what order should the visual symbols be introduced?
5 In what order and manner should children be taught to match the names and symbols?
6 When should children be taught to name the letters?
7 When should letter sounds be introduced and in what order?

Similar questions can be formulated regarding the various other beginning reading skills.

The search for a model of the beginning reading process which included a definitive list of subskills prerequisite to mastery of the decoding process by young children was disappointing. In the absence of such a model it was necessary to make a formal analysis of the reading process and define the subskill involved in beginning reading. This was undertaken in 1969 under the leadership of Dr R. G. Stennett, research psychologist and Chief of Educational Research Services with the London Board of Education, with a team composed of Dr H. R. Wilson, linguist, and Professor of English at the University of Western Ontario, Dr P. C. Smythe, psychologist, and Research Associate with the London Board of Education and the author as reading specialist. Financial support for the project came from the London Board of Education and the Canada Council.

Early in 1969 an exhaustive review of existing scientific knowledge about beginning reading was begun and is continuing. To date the research team has reviewed over 2,000 relevant research studies and these have been crossindexed in a variety of ways by computer.

*Pilot testing*
In May and June of 1970, two major projects were undertaken. The first consisted of administering a battery of eleven, newly developed tests to 200 children enrolled in kindergarten to grade three. The second project involved testing 100 children in grades one to four with a speech sound discrimination test. In October of 1970 about seventy-

five children in kindergarten and grade one were given revised versions of two tests from the original battery of eleven.

In January of 1971, twenty children enrolled in kindergarten to grade three were given pilot versions of sixteen newly developed or revised elemental skill tests. In addition, 100 children in grades three and four were given a series of pilot test items designed to assess their knowledge of lower-case letters. Between January and April a major project involving 100 children in grades one to four was done in the area of eye-movement. During May and June of 1971 sixteen tests were administered to 160 children in kindergarten to grade two.

A number of publications have been prepared which describe the findings of these pilot studies (Stennett *et al* 1971a, 1971b, 1971c, 1972a, 1972b; Smythe *et al* 1971a, 1971b; Hardy *et al* 1971, 1972a, 1972b). Only one of the studies will be discussed in any detail in this paper, i.e. phoneme discrimination.

*Phoneme discrimination*
As part of the pilot investigations, a detailed study of phoneme discrimination was conducted (Smythe *et al* 1972). Although auditory discrimination is generally accepted as a critical area in beginning reading, the relationship between auditory discrimination and beginning reading has not been extensively investigated. Typical studies of phoneme discrimination have used tests which required the subjects to make a judgment of similarity or difference between pairs of simple words or nonsense syllables. However, such studies have not been conducted at the level of the individual phoneme. The demands of what appears to be a simple test of phoneme discrimination are in fact complex, i.e. the child must listen to the two words or syllables being presented, retain these sounds in memory, make an internal comparison of them, and make a decision regarding their similarity or difference.

In order to reduce the complexity of the task and eliminate some of the memory complications, a test of auditory discrimination was constructed using the forty-two simplest sound elements in the English language and pairing them with each other. The test which resulted was made up of 1,291 pairs of phonemes, 861 of which were target items e.g. rŭ—gŭ, kŭ—vŭ, and 430 of which were buffer items e.g. rŭ—rŭ. The items were arranged in twenty-two subtests which were tape recorded and administered to 104 children enrolled in grades one to four in an elementary school. The tests were administered in a language laboratory on twenty-two consecutive school days, with testing time twelve minutes per class per day. Each day the children were required to listen to sixty phoneme pairs, make a judgment of similarity or difference, and record this decision on a simple preprinted answer sheet by making a check mark √ for similarity and x for difference.

Results of the testing indicated very high overall performance on the test at all grade levels, one to four. Nevertheless, there was a definite developmental trend, with increasing improvement in phoneme discrimination ability at each successive grade level. An analysis of errors indicated that very few phoneme pairs were contributing to the test difficulty. Contrary to a previous informal hypothesis that vowel-vowel pairs would give most difficulty, it appeared that difficult pairs were made up of consonants which were similar in place of articulation, e.g. $v-th_2$; $f-th_1$; $m-n-ng$. By the time children complete grade one, then, it appears that they experience very few phoneme discrimination difficulties, at the level of the individual phoneme. This suggests that with some of the popular tests of auditory discrimination, factors other than auditory discrimination ability are being measured, and exaggerated estimates of auditory discrimination difficulty are being made.

### 1971–72 phase of study

During the 1971–72 school year a battery of fourteen subtests was administered to 120 kindergarten and grade one children in three schools representing three different socioeconomic levels. These tests, administered initially in October, and repeated in February and June, represented the following areas: visual, auditory, visual/auditory, motor and memory/cognitive.

In order to relate the growth noted in the various reading skills tested to the reading instruction being given in the classroom, the nine teachers of the subjects of the study made a detailed monthly inventory of the reading instruction they gave.

An examination of the results of the October and February testing sessions, for two of the subtests, may be of interest.

### Auditory and visual language concepts

In learning to read, young children are confronted with a complicated array of auditory and visual language concepts which are an integral part of the instructional language used by primary teachers. Little is known of the normal development of these concepts, the order in which they should be introduced, and which of them should be mastered before critical reading skills are presented.

In the auditory area, children are often told to listen to words, sounds and letter names. Do they have the auditory concept of word, sound, and name of the letter? Which of these concepts is easiest? Primary children are also expected to identify differences in words, sounds etc, but do they have a firm concept of 'different'? Is it easier for them to understand 'different', 'not the same' or 'not alike'? The test of auditory language concepts which was developed to investigate fourteen auditory concepts was tape recorded and administered individually. Figure 1 contains results of the October 1971 and February 1972 tests and indicates the degree of mastery of the concepts which the children possessed early in kindergarten and grade one and how this mastery developed as instruction proceeded.

*Figure 1 Auditory Language Concepts*

| Concept | Percent of students with > 90% correct | | | |
|---|---|---|---|---|
| | Kindergarten | | Grade 1 | |
| | Oct. 71 | Feb. 72 | Oct. 71 | Feb. 72 |
| Beginning | 60 | 66 | 78 | 86 |
| Middle | 25 | 39 | 62 | 72 |
| End | 56 | 72 | 94 | 94 |
| First | 41 | 58 | 80 | 86 |
| Last | 44 | 78 | 90 | 88 |
| Different | 54 | 72 | 76 | 90 |
| Not alike | 31 | 62 | 66 | 78 |
| Not the same | 41 | 74 | 86 | 86 |
| Same | 46 | 88 | 82 | 88 |
| Alike | 58 | 92 | 92 | 96 |
| Rhyme | 13 | 46 | 56 | 74 |
| Word | 3 | 10 | 32 | 37 |
| Letter name | 21 | 49 | 60 | 66 |
| Sound (phoneme) | 0 | 2 | 3 | 10 |

The Visual Language Concepts Test explored the book-related and word-related concepts associated with beginning reading instruction. Questions such as the following formed the rationale for this test: Do young children need specific instruction in order to understand concepts such as page, cover, title, turn, top, side, word, letter, across? At what stage do children understand such word-related concepts as first, last, end, through, space, between, below, middle? The Visual Language Concepts Test was administered individually and required the children to identify nineteen book-related and twenty-one word-related elements. Figures 2 and 3 contain the results of this subtest.

*Figure 2 Visual Language Concepts*

*Percent of subjects answering correctly*

| Book-related concepts | Kindergarten | | Grade 1 | |
|---|---|---|---|---|
| | Oct. 71 | Feb. 72 | Oct. 71 | Feb. 72 |
| 1 book | 92 | 93 | 93 | 97 |
| 2 front | 82 | 93 | 99 | 98 |
| 3 title of book | 25 | 25 | 80 | 98 |
| 4 back | 75 | 95 | 98 | 99 |
| 5 cover | 74 | 85 | 92 | 97 |
| 6 page | 98 | 99 | 99 | 99 |
| 7 turn the page | 97 | 98 | 99 | 99 |
| 8 title of page | 13 | 20 | 80 | 95 |
| 9 bottom | 54 | 75 | 82 | 95 |
| 10 left side | 25 | 34 | 43 | 49 |
| 11 top | 66 | 75 | 68 | 81 |
| 12 right side | 28 | 37 | 42 | 56 |
| 13 line | 16 | 27 | 48 | 68 |
| 14 word | 31 | 64 | 87 | 99 |
| 15 letter | 72 | 92 | 93 | 99 |
| 16 capital letter | 34 | 39 | 78 | 90 |
| 17 across the page | 59 | 75 | 93 | 93 |
| 18 consonant | 10 | 07 | 03 | 10 |
| 19 vowel | 02 | 00 | 02 | 42 |

*Figure 3 Visual Language Concepts*

*Percent of subjects answering correctly*

| Word-related concepts | Kindergarten | | Grade 1 | |
| --- | --- | --- | --- | --- |
| | Oct. 71 | Feb. 72 | Oct. 71 | Feb. 72 |
| 1 under | 56 | 80 | 93 | 98 |
| 2 beside | 87 | 93 | 95 | 99 |
| 3 over | 95 | 95 | 93 | 99 |
| 4 below | 72 | 90 | 95 | 97 |
| 5 above | 75 | 90 | 92 | 97 |
| 6 on top of | 97 | 98 | 97 | 99 |
| 7 between | 72 | 86 | 98 | 99 |
| 8 box around | 67 | 86 | 98 | 99 |
| 9 circle around | 92 | 99 | 98 | 99 |
| 10 underline | 48 | 56 | 80 | 98 |
| 11 through | 74 | 88 | 97 | 97 |
| 12 last | 62 | 92 | 90 | 99 |
| 13 space between | 56 | 86 | 97 | 99 |
| 14 first | 57 | 88 | 93 | 99 |
| 15 end | 56 | 83 | 90 | 90 |
| 16 beginning | 48 | 76 | 87 | 93 |
| 17 middle | 75 | 93 | 93 | 95 |
| 18 little word | 59 | 75 | 98 | 98 |
| 19 long word | 67 | 81 | 98 | 99 |
| 20 big word | 69 | 80 | 93 | 99 |
| 21 short word | 46 | 61 | 83 | 93 |

*Mastery testing*
In order to allow the comparison of reading subskill development and reading mastery, the final testing session (June 1972) included three

mastery tests, i.e. silent reading (word recognition and comprehension), oral reading, and word attack.

The Word Attack Test was designed specifically for the study and the development offered an opportunity to conduct a pilot study of word attack ability of grades one and two children. It is fairly easy to specifically outline the *elements* of word attack but the *process* by which children analyse unknown words is poorly understood. Little is known of what children actually do when required to decode an unfamiliar word.

The pilot study of word attack attempted to have children describe the strategies which they used in decoding nonsense words designed around three main word analysis skills. Examples of test items in each of the three areas follow:

1  Comparison to known word: delp, hame, dowm
2  Structural analysis:
    i  Compound words: tryride, robinman, grassfriend
    ii  Little words in big: argo, seecoy, smand
    iii  Root word, prefix, suffix, inflectional ending: adnec, venly, naling
3  Phonic analysis and phonic generalizations: blar, fraip sime

The children were asked to 'read the funny words' and then to describe how they 'figured out what the funny words said'.

The children in the study experienced most success with the compound words subtest, followed by little words in big; comparison to known word; root word, prefix, suffix and inflectional ending; and phonics and phonic generalizations. The grade one and two children were able to describe the *process* they were using to attack unfamiliar words. Contrary to the hypothesis that each subtest would yield a distinctly different word attack strategy, essentially the same basic strategy was used in each subtest. This basic method was a consistent search for familiar words or word parts. Children who were successful in word attack were skilful in identifying known whole words or parts of words and then manipulating them by adding, deleting, substituting, and reordering. Responses such as the following were made: delp— 'Help has *l–p* at the end, so I put on the d and it says delp.'; woyj— 'It's like boy but it has a w plus a j.'

Attempts to improve children's power in word attack probably should be directed toward helping them achieve facility in manipulation of word parts. This undoubtedly involves the acquisition of strong auditory and visual concepts of each of those parts, and the ability to perform several operations with them. Basic operations appear to be identification, segmentation, decoding and blending of word parts. Additional useful procedures, as revealed in this study, include deletion, addition, substitution, and rearrangement of word parts. (Hardy *et al* 1972c)

*Future plans*
Analysis of the complete 1971–72 data should allow a reduction in the number of tests in the battery. Long-range plans call for the use of this refined and extended battery in following, on a longitudinal basis, a group of 300 children from kindergarten to the end of grade two.

The ultimate goal of the study is the development of a model of decoding which will provide the kind of information base upon which beginning reading tests and curriculum materials can be developed. Such tests and materials should allow for much more precision in the development of beginning reading skills than exists at present and for the prevention of many of the reading problems with which children and teachers are now plagued.

*References*
BETTS, E. A. (1971) Reading: graphic signals *The Reading Teacher* 25, 230–231
CHALL, J. (1967) *Learning To Read: The Great Debate* New York: McGraw-Hill
CROSBY, R. M. N. (1969) Recognizing the marks on paper *The Journal of Typographic Research* 3, 63–78
HARDY, M., SMYTHE, P. C., STENNETT, R. G. and WILSON, H. R. (1971) Developmental patterns in elemental reading skills: Phoneme-grapheme and grapheme-phoneme correspondences *Journal of Educational Psychology* 63, 5, 433–436
HARDY, M., SMYTHE, P. C., STENNETT, R. G. and WILSON, H. R. (1972a) Developmental patterns in elemental reading skills: Articulation (submitted to *Special Education in Canada*)
HARDY, M., STENNETT, R. G. and SMYTHE, P. C. (1972b) Auditory segmentation and auditory blending in relation to beginning reading (submitted to *Journal of Reading Behaviour*)
HARDY, M., STENNETT, R. G. and SMYTHE, P. C. (1972c) Word attack: How do they figure them out? (submitted to *The Reading Teacher*)
HUEY, E. B. (1908) *The Psychology and Pedagogy of Reading* New York: Macmillan
LEVIN, H. and WILLIAMS, J. P. (eds) (1970) *Basic Studies on Reading* New York: Basic Books
SMITH, N. B. (1961) What have we accomplished in reading? A review of the past fifty years *Elementary English* 3, 141–150

SMYTHE, P. C., STENNETT, R. G., HARDY, M. and WILSON, H. R. (1971a) Developmental patterns in elemental reading skills: Knowledge of upper-case and lower-case letter names *Journal of Reading Behaviour* 3, 24–33

SMYTHE, P. C., STENNETT, R. G., HARDY, M. and WILSON, H. R. (1971b) Developmental patterns in elemental reading skills: Visual discrimination of primary-type upper-case and lower-case letters *Journal of Reading Behaviour* 3, 6–13

SMYTHE, P. C., HARDY, M., STENNETT, R. G. and WILSON, H. R. (1972) Developmental patterns in elemental reading skills: Phoneme discrimination *Alberta Journal of Educational Research* 18, 59–67

STENNETT, R. G., SMYTHE, P. C. and THURLOW, M. (1971a) A pilot investigation of the relationship of eye movement measures to letter-printing and other elemental skills involved in learning to read *Special Education in Canada* 45, 27–30

STENNETT, R. G., SMYTHE, P. C., HARDY, M., WILSON, H. R. and THURLOW, M. (1971b) Developmental patterns in elemental reading skills: Preliminary report presented at *Reading 71*, York University

STENNETT, R. G., SMYTHE, P. C., HARDY, M. and WILSON, H. R., (1971c) Developmental patterns in elemental reading skills: Upper-case lower-case equivalences Board of Education (Mimeo) London: Ontario

STENNETT, R. G., SMYTHE, P. C., HARDY, M. and WILSON, H. R., (1972a) Developmental trends in letter-printing *Perceptual and Motor Skills* 34, 183–186

STENNETT, R. G., SMYTHE, P. C., PINKNEY, J. and FAIRBAIRN, A. (1972b) The relationship of eye movement measures to psychomotor skills and other elemental skills involved in learning to read (Submitted to *Journal of Reading Behaviour*)

VENEZKY, R. L. (1966) A study of selected grapheme-phoneme correspondence patterns *ERIC Project Literacy Report* 7

# 7  The ABCs of educational television - how's the reception?

*Shirley C. Feldmann*

Educators traditionally have been slow to incorporate products of technological advances into classroom procedures. The educational use of television has been no exception. Despite the twenty-five or so years of access to that medium, only in the last few years have educators employed any different educational formats in using television programming, that is formats other than those simulating traditional classroom methods of teaching.

In utilizing television for the teaching of reading to young children several problems may have impeded its widespread use. The first problem is how to get and hold the child's attention to the presentation on the screen. No teacher steps out of the television set to reinvolve the wandering mind or to change the emphasis or pace of the lesson when it seems not to suit the audience. The child is free to attend or not, perhaps without much regard for the quality of the presentation. Thus developmental reading programmes are likely to be in jeopardy if later lessons need to be based on previous ones.

A concomitant problem is that of feedback. There is no opportunity to ascertain whether the presentation has been learned or understood by the child. Whereas a teacher might spontaneously repeat a concept for needed emphasis, such programming decisions in television programmes have already been made and fixed at the time of production. Television programmes are geared to the group audience and therefore face the same problems as does the lecturer talking to a class of forty or more students.

Since the reading learner group as a whole is young, active, and widely varied in skill levels and learner styles, it has long been thought that television teaching of reading might be ineffective. Even so, several traditional reading programmes were presented as television programmes in the United States in past years. While they enjoyed mild success in their own areas, they were not widely adopted in other schools.

In recent years circumstances have coalesced to renew interest in the television teaching of reading. There has been widespread and vocal criticism of current educational practice and of apparently deteriorating schools. Considerable advice has been offered to educators, ranging from directives to abolish the schools altogether to returning to the good old traditions of a hundred years ago. Reading teaching has often been the major target of such critics because of its centrality to later school learning.

As part of a rejuvenation effort the United States Office of Education has mounted a ten-year effort, called The Right to Read, which has the stated purpose of eradicating illiteracy by 1980. Among the diverse programmes and approaches comprising The Right to Read effort was one providing the means and encouragement to develop a nationwide public television series to teach reading to children. It was hoped that such a series might provide new and creative educational approaches to an old and persistent problem, that of reading failure in young children.

The Children's Television Workshop, already known for their success in producing *Sesame Street*, the show for preschool children; took on the preparations for the new reading show. Two preliminary tasks were undertaken. The first one was to acquaint themselves with the present status of reading instruction. A large sample of specialists in diverse areas of education, psychology, psychiatry, and linguistics were interviewed or used as advisers for their views on reading and the task at hand. In addition, a review of all existing reading programmes was made to learn what programmes or materials had worked well in the past. Methods and materials were evaluated to see which might be particularly amenable to the television medium. An effort was made to discern which skills might be most crucial for successful reading learning.

While lack of strong empirical evidence as well as lack of consensus among the advisers precluded definitive answers to these questions, the ambiguity of the conclusions did provide support for use of a new and different format for teaching reading. The conclusion was that since there was no one best way to teach reading, newly devised ways might prove both effective and acceptable in a television series.

The second task was to delineate the characteristics of the series. Considering that the series was proposed for nationwide viewing, what should be the format of the show? To whom should the show be directed? Should it be produced for classroom or out of classroom use? What reading skills should be presented to the target audience and how should those skills be taught?

The format chosen for the series was an entertainment one. It was argued that entertainment shows were widely viewed and liked by young children, so a similar reading show could take advantage of many elements familiar to children and perhaps even preferred by children who had not made a successful start in school. A magazine-like format was selected which had a fast pace and featured rock music, comedy, animation, computer-generated graphics and the like. Such a format was, of course, unfamiliar to and untested in American education, and was one which was likely to arouse heated opinions.

Input from the advisers as well as from the survey of reading practices helped to select the target audience. It was designated as the seven to ten year old who has been exposed to reading instruction in the classroom but who, for a variety of reasons, has not progressed satisfactorily in reading. It has been estimated that a nationwide average of 30 per cent of the school children fall into this category, although in urban areas the proportion of poor readers might be as high as 60 to 70 per cent. The show thus was to become remedial in intent rather than developmental.

The show was set to be an extra classroom programme, providing enrichment supplementary to the regular classroom instruction, rather than replacing any classroom instruction. The series was intended to give the child who is weak in reading another chance to learn and to use reading skills by utilizing programmes with a highly appealing and less formal format than experienced in the classroom.

Because the thrust was to be remedial, the curriculum goals of the show were limited to the primary-level reading skills, usually taught in the first three grades of school. Since no continuity of viewing by the children could be assured, it was decided to disregard the developmental sequence among the skills to be represented. There was to be some grouping of skills within a programme but little or no hierarchical sequence was to be carried from one programme to another.

The curriculum itself was designed to stress certain basic understandings about reading. The primary one was that reading has a connection to speech and that the correspondences between these two are regular and discernible. It was planned to illustrate basic decoding principles with many examples so that the child could learn to apply such principles independently in his own reading. The ultimate goal of reading at all times was to get to the meaning of that which was read. For the young reader the decoding process was seen as a primary key to meaning; it was to be demonstrated there was an orderliness in that procedure that could aid the child. There was also a reasonableness about the rules of the code itself, despite the many exceptions in sound/symbol correspondence. All of these basic understandings, when translated into working procedures, were ultimately to furnish the child with a repertoire of skills which he could use for getting words and meanings from the printed page.

An important aspect of this do-it-yourself approach to reading was the fostering of the child's independence in reading. The underlying message to the child was that, having been provided with principles and procedures, he could proceed on his own to get the message or meaning from the print in front of him. The concept of *The Electric Company* providing 'power' to 'turn on' the child to reading was deliberately introduced to show the child that he too could learn the process of reading. The success thus engendered was hoped to help to revive his lagging motivation, a by-product of his previous failures with reading.

In describing the specific skills of the reading curriculum they fall into two areas: those that provide strategies for sound/symbol analysis and those that give the child a better understanding of what connected reading is. The decoding skills to be presented included consonant and vowel sounds, blending, letter groups or chunks such as *oo, ight,* or *alk,* and scanning for structure, such as the silent e and s as possessive or plural. Context clues, punctuation and spoken patterns were included to illustrate aids in reading larger connected units.

The curriculum was so organized that each show featured several areas illustrated in diverse ways. Segments were reviewed in successive shows but with no specific continuity built in. As mentioned earlier, there was no developmental sequence planned for the series so that understanding the content of one show was not dependent on having seen a previous show.

As to be expected, the curriculum featured no one method or style of teaching reading. The remedial approach chosen was more amenable to the so-called 'cafeteria approach' which utilized varying methods appropriate to a particular skill and the format of the episode in which it was presented. As a safeguard, there was review of the various episodes by educational advisers to make sure that whatever the reading approach used it was used consistently and accurately.

The completed series consisted of 130 half-hour shows which were presented five days a week from October until the end of April. Each day the show was seen once during school hours and then again at 5.30, directly following *Sesame Street*. On Saturdays the week's five shows were reshown, alternating with the *Sesame Street* shows. Although the show was primarily intended for out of school viewing, surveys showed that over 18,000 schools, or about 40 per cent of those having access to stations showing *The Electric Company,* were tuning in during school hours. Later surveys showed however, that after-school watching was increasing, although it still did not surpass the in-school viewing.

The first year's series of *The Electric Company* has been completed. How has the reception been? A number of questions could be asked concerning the show's effectiveness. Did the children learn the skills that were presented? Did they like the show? How did teachers respond to the show? How did the Workshop staff and advisers respond to the translation of their earlier concepts into programme episodes? For a preliminary evaluation of *The Electric Company,* four separate sources of information have been gathered: reports of studies of viewer achievement; data from a teacher questionnaire; reports of informal classroom observations; and advisers' evaluations.

Studies of viewer achievement were undertaken both by the Workshop's research staff and by an outside agency, the Educational Testing Service. In these studies the reading skills of second and third grade children who viewed special showings of the series in their own classrooms were contrasted with those of nonviewers from comparable classes. Children in schools in two communities viewed thirty consecutive shows over a six-week period. Pretests, covering specific skills to be featured in the thirty shows, were administered to both groups. Similar posttests, administered after the viewing period, provided the contrast scores for both groups. Results showed that the viewers, as opposed to the nonviewers, made gains in many skill areas. The largest gains were made in areas of consonant blends, final e, punctuation, and reading words from sentences. Thus there were indications that skills presented in the series were learned by the children who viewed the show and that those gains were larger than gains for nonviewers. The results came from studies of only several hundred children. Large-scale studies only recently completed will give more substantial evidence about reading skill learning.

The second source of information was from data from a teacher questionnaire, which had been sent to a random sample of those teachers who had subscribed to the teachers' guide for the show, and thus who were probably viewing the show with their classes during school hours. The majority of teachers answered affirmatively to questions concerning their pupils' interest in the show. Generally, the teachers observed that children responded actively to the series and further, that their pupils' interest in reading had increased with continued viewing.

In responding to the curriculum, teachers felt the most effective segments of the show were those that the children found the most appealing. Also there was felt to be some correlation between the effectiveness in presenting skills in a particular curriculum area and the amount of emphasis that area received on the show, that is, frequency of presentation seemed to be a factor in the amount of skill learning observed. There was general agreement that the curriculum areas covered in the series were those crucial to beginning reading instruction. On the whole then, the teachers sampled were positive to the aims of the show and to its observed effects on their pupils.

Informal classroom observations, the third source of input concerning the effectiveness of *The Electric Company,* were carried out by Workshop staff as well as by advisers. Observation reports covered such a variety of areas and situations that it is difficult to generalize about the results. It was observed that many children seemed to be positively oriented toward the show and seemed attracted by the music and the attention-getting devices used. Children who were questioned by observers felt that they were learning to read from the show.

All observers emphasized that the individual teacher seemed to set the tone for reading instruction in the classroom and therefore the use

E

that she made of *The Electric Company* seemed to be in direct proportion to her views of its value to her own reading lessons. Thus some teachers incorporated the series into their own lessons while others substituted it wholly for their lessons, and still others used it only for supplementary entertainment. Since no evaluation of the amount of the children's learning under these varied circumstances was obtained, the value of such diverse uses remains to be explored.

The last source of comments came from the educational advisers who had helped to plan the curriculum and format the preceding year, and who gathered together at the close of the series for discussion and evaluation of it. There was some unease among this group concerning the fast pace and frenetic quality of the show, even though those elements seemed to be attractive to many of the children. Advisers questioned whether the skill levels and pace were too difficult for the youngest group, the seven year olds, and so requested that there be more low-level skills presented, with frequent repetition for the slowest learners.

They strongly requested more emphasis on reading for meaning, feeling that the show concentrated too much on decoding skills and thus belied the concept of decoding as a tool to get to meaning. They asked to have underlined and reinforced the concept that reading is also done in books and that books contain valuable and enriching ideas. A slight deemphasis on decoding with more stress on reading content and ideas was preferred. Suggestions were also made for reinforcement and extension of reading skills through supplying supplementary materials such as books, games and records. It is thus expected in the coming year that comprehension will be stressed more in the show and there will be an extension of learning opportunities through publication of additional reading materials.

In summary, the evaluations described give varying degrees of evidence that *The Electric Company* is indeed 'turning on' the children and helping them to learn reading skills. Larger questions of its long-term impact on reading skills of the young learner, of its effect on continued motivation to read and learn, and its impact on the child's functional use of reading skills to understand, evaluate, and think will take more time to answer. The show seems to have met its preliminary goals of being exciting to children, of satisfying teachers and reading experts, and of teaching some reading skills. Thus, the reception to date seems good.

# 8 Developing flexibility of reading rate

*Lawrence W. Carrillo*

Years ago, in collaboration with Sheldon, the author published an article outlining various factors necessary in order to design a testing instrument for flexibility of reading rate (Carrillo and Sheldon 1952). Recently, Steinacher (1971) has quoted this older article as a partial rationale for his point of view: that we cannot really teach flexibility of rate since we are not sure what it is, but should instead concentrate on more careful specification of tasks. It is the purpose here, therefore, to define and further clarify the concept of flexibility.

Flexibility of reading rate is the skill of not reading everything in the same manner. It is that characteristic which enables a reader to vary his rate according to his task and his taste. Relatively few readers do this. It is a truly mature level of reading skill, probably not to be reached by all who read. In the interests of efficiency, however, flexibility of reading rate is most certainly badly needed by many, because of the knowledge explosion and the fact that we are all limited to only twenty-four hours a day.

In order to achieve this mature level of reading skill, at least three things are necessary:

1 The reader must first have established the basic comprehension and vocabulary skills.
2 The reader must keep his purpose always in mind.
3 The reader must know how to speed up and feel free to do so when it suits his purpose and his level of comprehension.

## Comprehension

The many studies correlating comprehension and rate are contradictory and essentially meaningless, as Harris (1968) points out in his summary. Perhaps the reason for this is so obvious that it did not even occur to those doing the studies: insofar as the approach to reading is flexible, rate and comprehension will vary together. If the ideas are easily assimilated and the purpose is being easily met, rate will increase; where difficulty is found, the opposite will occur. This is an *individual* situation, not particularly amenable to correlational study.

Understanding vocabulary is essential, so that the words met in reading will be familiar and readily recognized for the most part. 'Strange' words slow the reader down to a decoding process. First he must 'call' the word; then he must search the context for clues to the meaning. Both of these processes are antithetical to real speed, since they have to do with a single word and not ideas as expressed in larger units of print. This is, however, one aspect of flexibility—the reader must realize that he *must slow down* and go through this process in order to continue to comprehend. He must always be *conscious of his level of understanding* of the printed passage. When the reader senses a loss of understanding, he slows down, rereads, or takes other steps to increase comprehension, any of which will decrease the rate until understanding has again been achieved. If, on the other hand, he finds the material easy to understand or if his purpose, for example, is to find only a few significant details, he should probably increase his speed considerably.

All of this means that instruction in basic comprehension, so that *one knows how much one knows* when reading, is a prerequisite to flexibility.

### Purpose

The importance of purpose as a regulator of speed in reading is that if you know what you want when you start out, you are much more likely to attain it. Knowing your purpose in reading a selection removes much of the inefficiency of 'trial and error'. An older study by Moe and Nania (1959) shows this; they made students aware of purpose by having the students first read the questions to be answered later (a tried and true study method). Significant gains in flexibility resulted.

However, there is evidence from the examination of published tests and from various comments in the literature, that we have not been very clear in our statements of purpose. Purpose statements to the reader, if given at all, are generally vague and mostly concerned only with difficulty level, rather than type of understanding necessary. Nicholaw (1969) found that the length and the difficulty of the material are not as important as the purpose set, and significantly differentiated two particular purposes:

1　careful reading for main ideas
2　rapid reading for significant details.

He also emphasized the need for practice of flexibility with carefully designed exercises of these two types.

Until teachers learn to give specific purposes, and until materials carefully stating purposes are available, the problem of reading for purpose is likely to be the major problem in the development of flexible reading.

### Improving rate

Due to commercial interests in 'speed' reading, associated with mechanical devices promoted as rate builders, and because of continuing research on perceptual and attitudinal skills in reading, the area of reading rate has been quite controversial in the past decade.

To attempt to clarify the situation for the teaching profession, authorities such as Spache (1962) pointed out that while rates of several thousand words per minute can be attained while utilizing *skimming* procedures, lines of print are likely to be totally ignored. Genuine reading, in which almost all the words *are* perceived, cannot be achieved at a rate faster than 800 to 900 words per minute in view of the known physiological limits. This conclusion, supported by others, uses data which show that the shortest possible fixation in reading two to three words is at least a fifth to a quarter of a second in duration. This would mean that a ten word line would be read in two thirds of a second. Speeds, therefore, which exceed 900 words per minute must be achieved by *skipping,* not only words, but lines and blocks of print. Very obviously, this can only result in decreased comprehension, and represents a type of locational skill rather than reading.

Those who can make claims for the efficiency of machines in the teaching of reading usually speak about eye movements and their development. Efficient eye movements, few and short fixation pauses, and a good return sweep to the next line are *symptoms* of good reading. Good readers show these symptoms, but a person who develops more efficient eye movements or faster perceptions while using a machine will not necessarily become a good reader. Using a machine that increases the perception span may help a person see more at one fixation *while using the machine,* but unless provision is made for transfer of the skill to the printed page, the increased machine-perception span may serve no practical purpose. By itself a mechanistic approach will not ordinarily result in lasting gains, but the machine may act as a motivating device or as proof to the student of his own potential. Still, any machine used should approximate the natural reading situation as far as possible.

With regard to machines as aids to reading instruction, most authorities and studies agree with Berger (1966), who states in his summary: '... whatever can be done by machine can be done equally as well—if not better—(and cheaper) without'.

It is in the area of perceptual and attitudinal correlates of rate that much more needs to be done. Glass (1967) completed an important study which indicated that rate of perception and knowledge of vocabulary were rather highly related to reading rate. A significant *negative* correlation was found between compulsiveness and rate. Not quite as highly related, but still significantly related to rate, were speed of closure and flexibility of closure. These perceptual factors and the one attitudinal factor of compulsiveness deserve greater consideration in the research.

Attention can be, and should be, given in the research and in the classroom to the concept of cue reduction. At the stage where flexibility of rate can be developed, we are no longer concerned with decoding, but rather with rapidity of *visual* discrimination of word and phrase forms. In fact, it is easily possible that too much attention in the early stages of reading instruction to phonics, structural analysis, structural linguistics, and/or oral reading, will interfere later with flexibility of rate. It would seem an even greater possibility when this type of overdone instruction appears in conjunction with certain characteristics of individual personality such as compulsiveness and perfectionism (Carrillo 1965).

Instead of the sounds in words, then, we might more profitably consider such word form characteristics and cues as:

1 *Beginnings of words*—they contribute much more to recognition than endings.
2 *Ascending and descending letters*—vowels for example, lack visual form.
3 *The top half of print*—in the English language, the top portion of printed words leads to much easier identification than does the bottom half.
4 *Use of lower-case and manuscript writing*—material printed all in capitals is more difficult to read.
5 *Spacing*—spaces between words are significant determiners of rate and comprehension.
6 *Closure*—the effect of closure on recognition may be tested by the use of broken type. This could also be a teaching method in cue reduction which, as far as is known, has not been used.
7 *Rearrangement of print* in certain situations—perhaps, where rapid recognition is imperative (such as highway signs) we should consider the rearrangement of English print into blocks or vertical arrangements, as suggested by Schale (1965).

Many other suggestions might be made here for ways to improve rate of reading and therefore the chances for flexibility (Fry 1963; Carrillo 1965), but the important point is this: rates of reading for any mature reader should vary from a 'floor' corresponding to a slow speed of speech to some 'ceiling' controlled only by his speed of thinking as based on the print he perceives. In order to achieve the possibility of many rates of reading (flexibility) applied at any moment (McCracken 1965), the individual must first develop considerable distance between his reading floor and ceiling. Then, with this room available, he must be *taught* flexibility.

*References*
BERGER, A. (1966) Selected review of studies on the effectiveness of various methods of increasing reading efficiency *Journal of the Reading Specialist* 6, 74–87

CARRILLO, L. W. and SHELDON, W. D. (1952) The flexibility of reading rate *Journal of Educational Psychology* 43, 299–305

CARRILLO, L. W. (1965) Developing flexible reading rates *Journal of Reading* 8, 322–325

FRY, E. (1963) *Teaching Faster Reading* London: Cambridge University Press

GLASS, G. G. (1967) Rate of reading: a correlation and treatment study *Journal of Reading* 11, 168–177

HARRIS, A. J. (1968) Research on some aspects of comprehension: Rate, flexibility and study skills *Journal of Reading* 12, 205–210, 258–259

HILL, W. (1968) 'Applying research findings in rate of reading to classroom practice (secondary)' in H. Figurel (ed) *Forging Ahead in Reading* Newark: International Reading Association

McCRACKEN, R. A. (1965) Internal versus external flexibility of reading rate *Journal of Reading* 8, 208–9

MOE, L. and NANIA, F. (1959) Reading deficiences among able pupils *Journal of Developmental Reading* 3, 11–26

NICHOLAW, A. (1969) *Reading for Purpose: Instruction and Practice Effects on Rate, Comprehension and Flexibility* Unpublished doctoral dissertation, Syracuse University

PAUK, W. (1970) Can the mind speed read? *Journal of the Reading Specialist* 10, 14–18

SCHALE, F. (1965) Vertical methods of increasing rate of comprehension *Journal of Reading* 8, 296–300

SPACHE, G. D. (1962) Is this a breakthrough in reading? *The Reading Teacher* 15, 258–263

STEINACHER, R. (1971) Reading flexibility: Dilemma and solution *Journal of Reading* 16, 143–50

WITTY, P. (1969) Rate of reading—a crucial issue *Journal of Reading* 13, 102–106, 154–163

# 9  Extending reading efficiencies

*William A. Gatherer*

Assuming that 'reading efficiency' is too monolithic a term for an activity so complex and many-sided as reading, this paper suggests three different efficiencies *reading as process, literate reading* and *strategic literate reading,* and suggests some of the teaching approaches for each. The theoretical model on which the descriptions are based is that which is emerging from the work of cognitive psychologists and psycholinguists. A number of expositions of the model, or parts of it, may be found in Goodman (1968), Levin and Williams (1970) and Smith (1971). In none of these, however, is there discussion of the educational efficiencies dealt with here.

Briefly, the theory sees the act of reading as the perception of distinctive features in text, a distinctive feature being a characteristic of shape or size which serves as the crucial distinguishing mark between two items, for example between letters, phonemes, graphemes or words. It is claimed that for the experienced reader no more than five distinctive features are theoretically sufficient to distinguish all the letters of the alphabet, and that a word can be identified from many thousands of alternatives by means of about a dozen features (Smith 1971). As his reading skills develop, the child assembles mental features lists which enable him to assign visual configurations to meaning categories. When he can allocate a configuration (a letter, or a word, or a group of letters or words) to a named category in his feature list, he can identify it immediately. If he has no feature list appropriate for a given configuration, he can have recourse to mediated identification: in the case of a letter this might merely be asking what it is; in the case of a word it might be by phonic analysis and sounding out the word. The skilled reader can identify almost every word he meets immediately (which means without mediation, not instantaneously.)

Just as there are two ways of identifying words, that is through immediate categorization or through the mediation of identifying letters or clusters and 'putting them together', so there are two ways of reading for comprehension; mediated comprehension which requires the prior identification of separate words, and immediate comprehension, which involves going straight from the visual information to the meaning.

The distinction between reading as process and literate reading is crucial for teachers, for confusing the two efficiencies can lead to frustration and wasted time. Reading as process is identifying by reading the linguistic forms which can be identified by hearing (Reed 1970). Sounding out a word rarely helps in identifying its meaning: it merely changes the input channel. Perception of meaning by listening is itself a process of identification, prediction and the application of prior knowledge (Johnson-Laird 1970). It is only occasionally that the translation of graphemic substance into acoustic substance will help the mature reader; to put it another way, it is not often that one knows the meaning of a word when one hears it but not when one sees it written. In general children must learn to do without the mediating operation if they are to learn to read fluently.

The young pupil's problems are first, his lack of speed in identifying words: second, his lack of confidence in responding to a text; third, his general linguistic immaturity. These three deficiencies are, as we shall see, closely related to one another.

Normal reading cannot proceed by a letter-by-letter serial scan (Kolers 1970). If meaning is to be held by the long-term memory, it is essential that four or five words should be assimilated into the short-term memory at any one time. (You can confirm this by getting someone to read out a passage in a monotone at a word per second. You have to keep repeating words subvocally to retain them in groups of four or five, but it is difficult to retain the meaning of the passage at the same time (Smith 1971).) It is therefore important for the beginner to acquire speed in identification, and for this he needs practice in the process of feature analysis. The best way (perhaps the only effective way) of providing this practice to the beginner is letting him read aloud and giving him ample feedback. In the one-to-one teaching situation the child can hazard responses continuously and test his hypotheses instantly. It is not, of course, necessary for the teacher to verbalize his signals—a nod or keeping silent can be just as meaningful. A child may make partial identifications more often than the teacher realizes. Unfortunately it often happens that the only way he can signal uncertainty is by saying nothing, so that the teacher cannot provide help. Occasionally a pupil may venture a bit of a word—for example the segment *no* in 'nothing'—and be stuck there. The teacher should supply the whole word at once and encourage the pupil to go on and get the gist of the sentence or passage. Children should be encouraged to expect feedback of this kind, for it is vital to success in process reading. Parents are often convinced that their children are better at reading than the teacher says: this may well be because the child is more relaxed at home and readier to offer partial or whole identifications.

Practice in the process of reading should be obtained by pupils at all stages. For those who have already mastered the early techniques, reading easy fiction provides valuable practice: the story line not only sustains interest, it also provides feedback since it would not hold the child's attention unless he were successfully extracting the meaning from the text. Teachers sometimes condemn pulp fiction for children for the thinness of its content, but it does offer an early opportunity for the development of fluent reading.

A pupil's lack of confidence in responding to a text will be increased by an excessive concern for correctness. We learn from signal detection theory that in any process of continuous identification the perceiver sets his own criterion: either he wishes to minimize error or he wishes to maximize success. He cannot do both at the same time: if he sets out to make as few mistakes as possible, he will make fewer correct responses because he will want more information before he makes a decision; if he sets out to maximize his correct responses he will also increase the number of errors he makes (Smith 1971). The beginner in reading should be encouraged to set his criterion low, that is to opt for making many successful identifications even at the cost of also making many false identifications. In reading, as in other activities, nothing succeeds like success. Reading requires speed; speed requires the willingness to take chances; confident guesswork relies upon plentiful feedback.

Linguistic maturity is an important factor in reading efficiencies. It is now well established that children have developed a certain communicative competence before they start school (Halliday *et al* 1964; Boyle 1971). While little is known about the relationship between linguistic experience and reading, it is certain that success in reading is at least partly dependent upon competence in the other linguistic skills (Vernon 1971). For many children, learning to read carries a double load of effort: if their natural sound-system is different from that of the classroom, they are expected to learn to use the 'standard' variety of the language as well as to process the information into speech (Labov 1970). Thus it is important for the teacher to have regard for the general linguistic experience of the pupils during the early learning stages. Hence the desirability of conversation, discussion, story-telling, drama and other language activities. Even at a later stage, when pupils have mastered the early techniques, the use of projects and other interdisciplinary programmes of work ensures that the linguistic forms being encountered in their reading are reinforced in the course of other linguistic experiences.

Literate reading is the extraction of meaning from text without the intervention of mediating operations such as phonic synthesis or vocalization. Unlike the beginner, the literate reader does not pay attention to letters or syllabic clusters unless he has instructed himself to do so. Normally, he moves as it were directly from the visual array to the meaning. Reed postulates the interposition of 'linguons' or segments of linguistic forms, but even in that case the process is one of unmediated thought-getting (Reed 1970). The differences between reading as process and literate reading are dramatized by the use of the term 'mechanics' for the one activity and Neisser's definition of the other as 'externally guided thinking' (Neisser 1967).

Literate reading is made possible by the phenomenon of redundancy in text. This may be defined as the excess of linguistic signals above the minimum that can carry a message (Gleason 1965). It is, to put it more simply, the splendid liberality of clues to meaning that language possesses. Words contain more informational redundancy than letters do, and can be identified even when their component letters are singly unidentifiable. This is because the redundancy reduces the amount of featural information that needs to be discriminated in any letter position to less than the amount of information needed to identfy the letter itself in isolation. For example you can identify p in 'chip' more easily than you can identify p by itself because (to mention only two of the distinctive features involved) there are very few letters that could occur in that particular position, and in fact none at all other than p that also have a downward stroke. There are many forms of redundancy in language, but the most potent form in the reading process is sequential redundancy: that is, the evidence that enables you, from your natural knowledge of grammar, to predict how a construction will proceed and complete itself.

The literate reader samples a text not by identifying, say, one word in four, but by sampling the features available along the whole line of text (Smith 1971). In some way that is not yet fully understood, he interprets the surface structure of the language to grasp the underlying relationships of meaning in the deep structure. (For an explanation of deep and surface structure, see Thomas 1965). One of the resources which makes this possible is the great amount of linguistic knowledge he brings to the text. It has been suggested that the skilled reader constructs meaning rather as the archeologist constructs the past—from fragmentary evidence and a lot of general knowledge (Neisser 1967). As Roger Brown (1970) has pointed out:

> In a very general sense, the skilled reader knows in advance a large proportion of what is in any new text; he knows what is there because he knows English, he knows writers, and he knows about the world.

The better one knows a subject the easier it is to read about it, simply because predicting comes more easily when you are familiar with the linguistic forms you are encountering as you read. It is for this reason, perhaps, that some children love to read a book they know well.

The improvement of literate reading efficiency is a matter of developing speed without sacrificing comprehension. In literate reading speed is a characteristic of the rate at which the information can be taken in, and this varies with the reader's cognitive abilities and the difficulty of the material read. As teachers are continually being told, they must try to fit the book to the reader, not the other way round (Central Committee on English 1967; 1968; 1971). One of the most important characteristics of the thematic approach in teaching is that it encourages pupils to read material that is part of their other cognitive and sensory experiences.

The highly skilled literate reader has developed the ability to read strategically. The mature reader conducts a kind of dialogue with the text (Melnik, 1971):

> ... continually, if often subconsciously, the reader or listener is asking himself questions and finding answers, sometimes tentative answers which are accepted until a conclusive one can be formed. ... Reading is intelligent in direct proportion to the number of questions asked by the reader.

The strategies adopted vary according to what one is reading for, one's knowledge of the subject domain, one's knowledge of the writer's intention, style and habits of thought. In a confrontation with a text one has to pay attention to various aspects of its structure: the rhetorical structure of the whole work, the syntactical and logical structure of each paragraph, the grammatical and punctuational structure of the sentence, the morphological structure of the less familiar words (Central Committee on English 1971). Each structural aspect suggests heuristics or tactics as to the reading methodology to be adopted: thus in the act of reading one is continually changing gear, varying one's speed, one's method of scanning, one's degree of attention and so on. A text contains what might be termed stylistic and dialectic redundancy i.e. evidence which points the reader towards making the best practical use of the text which indicates whether it should, in Bacon's well-known terms, be tasted, swallowed, or chewed and digested, or whether it should not in fact be studied at all but 'read by deputy'.

It is difficult to conceive of any new teaching method whereby these skills could be systematically inculcated. The only means at the teacher's disposal is to read and discuss a text along with his pupils, pointing out the devices which the separation by time and space compel the writer to use, and suggesting reading devices by which the reader can complete the act of communication. This 'close reading' or 'reading together' lesson can be an invaluable experience for the literate pupil, provided that the teacher is skilled enough and sufficiently highly cultured to analyse the work in the depth required (Calthrop 1971). Unfortunately in the secondary schools the only teachers who attempt this type of lesson are teachers of English, and even these do not appear to do it very often (Whitehead 1966; Squire and Applebee 1969). One suspects that there is even less done in the primary schools. It is only too probable that the majority of teachers do not possess the skills required for effective close reading techniques; but even a little training could produce valuable results. As the Newsom Report puts it (Central Advisory Council for Education 1963):

> No amount of training would have enabled William Bunter to defeat Roger Bannister on the track. None the less a trained Bunter could have knocked one or two minutes off the time of an untrained Bunter for the mile.

This applies equally to teachers and to pupils.

There can be little doubt that what is called a 'reading drive' by Southgate (1972) and a 'developmental reading programme' in the United States would, if well planned and faithfully carried out, improve all three of the efficiencies discussed here. But the status and function of such a programme would have to be made appropriate to the aims and methods of the modern school: it is not enough merely to substitute amateur enthusiasm for professional indifference. We shall have to reconsider the concept of developmental reading, and in particular investigate the means whereby methodical teaching of the skills can be fitted into the syllabuses of the content subjects. When teachers of the social subjects or mathematics or science start planning reading programmes within their own disciplines, when the whole of a primary school staff meet regularly to plan an integrated developmental sequence of activities, when the colleges of education make the teaching of reading a compulsory subject for every student, then we shall begin to see real progress.

*References*

BOYLE, D. G. (1971) *Language and Thinking in Human Development* London: Hutchinson

BROWN, R. (1970) 'Psychology and reading' in H. Levin and J. P. Williams (ed) *Basic Studies on Reading* New York: Basic Books

CALTHROP, K. (1971 *Reading Together* London: Heinemann

CENTRAL ADVISORY COUNCIL FOR EDUCATION (1963) *Half Our Future* (Newsom Report) London: HMSO

CENTRAL COMMITTEE ON ENGLISH (1967) *English in the Secondary School—Early Stages* Edinburgh: HMSO

CENTRAL COMMITTEE ON ENGLISH (1968) *The Teaching of Literature* Edinburgh: HMSO

CENTRAL COMMITTEE ON ENGLISH (1971) *English in the Secondary School—Later Stages* Edinburgh: HMSO

GLEASON, H. A. (1965) *Linguistics and English Grammar* New York: Holt, Rinehart and Winston

GOODMAN, K. S. (1968) (ed) *The Psycholinguistic Nature of the Reading Process* Detroit: Wayne State University Press

HALLIDAY, M. A. K., MCINTOSH, A. and STEVENS, P. (1964) *The Linguistic Sciences and Language Teaching* London: Longman

JOHNSON-LAIRD, P. N. (1970) 'The perception and memory of sentences' in J. Lyons (ed) *New Horizons in Linguistics* Harmondsworth: Penguin

KOLERS, P. A. (1970) 'Three stages of reading' in H. Levin and J. P. Williams (eds) *Basic Studies on Reading* New York: Basic Books

LABOV, W. (1970) *The Study of Nonstandard English* Champaign: NCTE

LEVIN, H. and WILLIAMS, J. P. (1970) (eds) *Basic Studies on Reading* New York: Basic Books

MELNIK, A. (1971) 'Reading as a thought-getting process' in J. Merritt (ed) *Reading and the Curriculum* London: Ward Lock Educational

NEISSER, U. (1967) *Cognitive Psychology* New York: Appleton-Century-Crofts

REED, D. W. (1970) 'Linguistic forms and the process of reading' in H. Levin and J. P. Williams (eds) *Basic Studies on Reading* New York: Basic Books

SMITH, F. (1971) *Understanding Reading* New York: Holt, Rinehart and Winston

SOUTHGATE, V. (1972) *Beginning Reading* London: University of London Press

SQUIRE, J. R. and APPLEBEE, R. K. (1969) *Teaching English in the United Kingdom* Champaign: NCTE

THOMAS, O. (1965) *Transformational Grammar and the Teacher of English* New York: Holt, Rinehart and Winston

VERNON, M. D. (1971) *Reading and its Difficulties* London: Cambridge University Press

WHITEHEAD, F. (1966) *The Disappearing Dais* London: Chatto and Windus

# 10 Bridging the gap between children's book people and reading people

*Richard Bamberger*

The importance of children's books is frequently stressed by those interested in reading. The teacher for her part highlights the need for a good supply of children's books for the acquisition of successful reading skills, and the children's book expert regards improved reading ability as an important factor if children are to enjoy books. Every teacher realizes the importance of books and the role of the library, yet in the classroom she too often employs only the official textbooks and makes no use of the wealth of reading material available. Closer investigation usually reveals that many teachers appreciate children's books only in theory; in practice they may have read only a few of them—a long time ago—and may be unable to talk enthusiastically to their pupils about books they might enjoy at a certain age and under certain circumstances. Librarians, on the other hand, know about the importance of effective reading, of reading with ease and understanding, of a certain speed in reading that correlates with the readability of the reading material and about the importance of critical and creative reading, but too often they recommend to young people children's books that are far beyond their reading level, and are then surprised that these children read only reluctantly and soon stop reading completely. Thus librarians usually only reach the born readers, or 'environmental' readers, but not those who are most in need of the help books can give them for their personal growth.

What applies to the individual teacher or the individual librarian is also true of his organizations. Theoretically, the associations of librarians and of teachers of reading hold each other in high esteem. However, on closer investigation you will find that members of one group do not know who is the president of the other group; nor about their congresses; nor are they familiar with the professional literature of the other group. Thus there is rarely cooperation of a practical kind or joint action in furthering their common aims. It seems that the good opinion reading people and children's book people have of one another is not enough. The teacher must realize that even her pupils who have successfully mastered reading skills may often fail to develop into permanent lifelong readers. Very often a teacher of reading is very proud of her success, but it does not occur to her that she may have to thank somebody else for this result. The great German dramatist Gerhart Hauptmann has expressed it in this way: 'I did not learn to read at school but through Robinson and Cooper's *Leather Stockings*.' One does not learn reading solely by being trained in reading skills but also by experiencing the 'practice effect' of a great many children's books. Both teachers and librarians must go beyond their traditional opinions and beliefs in the field of reading and come to face facts.

It is important for research to study not only reading at school but the totality of the child's reading.

*Standards and Progress in Reading* (Morris 1966) has helped research in Austria. Using the experience of that study it has been possible to go beyond its scope and include not only the reading standards achieved but also the reading and book situation in practical life.

The following are the main points considered in our study:

1 The percentage of children and adults in a given area who may be regarded as permanent book readers: that is with how many children we are successful in the school situation, and how many of them usually remain readers in later life.

2 The number and kind of books read in a certain period both by children in experimental classes, who are given help and a variety of reading material, and by children in ordinary classes, that is control classes.

3 The measurement of reading ability in terms of speed, comprehension, critical approach and aesthetic appreciation.

4 The extent to which the amount of reading a child does is reflected in reading ability, personal growth and educational or academic output.

It is hoped that the results of this study will convince both the teacher and the librarian of the importance of cooperation. It may also help to persuade the authorities to make more generous provision for reading material for school libraries.

The change in the reading situation according to the volume of reading done by children is one of the best yardsticks for the success of the work of the teachers and the librarians. Such a study should from time to time be carried out by scientific institutes or professional organizations and not be left only to individual teachers and librarians or even local communities. The teachers will be convinced to a certain extent by the results of such studies. The greatest conviction will however be gained from their own experiences. In Vienna, we have developed a simple device which we feel will help teachers, the *reader passport*. It is a method introduced to the class by the teacher herself for measuring reading achievement, and trains the pupil to measure his own, very individual reading achievement, offering also a clear motivation for improvement.

The passport consists of a monthly notation of individual test results and a survey of currently read books.

Both reading speed and comprehension are, to a great extent, the result of practice. With the use of the reader passport the pupil learns that the results of the monthly tests improve proportionally with the number of books read. The first reading tests in Austria were meant as objective achievement measures for the teachers. The pupils however showed great interest in the tests and those who had previously shown little interest in reading changed their attitude and suddenly attempted to read better because of the objective 'score' attained in reading speed and comprehension. The pupils were given a concentrated reading programme, as well as regular tests, to help them see their improvement. The positive effects of tests have been verified in other countries, where even weekly achievement measurements have been used.

Our tests for the reader passport have been specially developed to assess both speed and comprehension. The multiple-choice type tests are scored on a hundred point basis by the pupils themselves immediately upon completion. The tests can be taken by the pupil alone at home, and experience has shown that children who have reached the third or fourth year of school are often delighted to test themselves and note their individual progress. This makes the method especially suitable for use in reading clubs for example. In order that the children learn to have confidence in the method and to enjoy the exercises, the first tests are rather short and quite easy so that every child can do as well as possible. Later the degree of difficulty is increased and different tests are given to various groups according to their achievement level. Text selection is especially important. The texts read and used for testing speed and comprehension must correspond to the pupil's achievement level; the demand must not be too great. In testing the whole class, very simple texts are used; for small groups, texts are of various levels of difficulty. At present we use inexpensive booklets of excerpts which are available from the Austrian Children's Book Club and which also offer an added motivation to read the complete text.

From the viewpoint of motivation, it has been found valuable to use the beginning of a complete text. If, however, one wants to give the children practice in comprehending the essential details, a central part which is complete within itself is more appropriate. Complete stories, especially sagas or short nonfiction may also be used. Parts of a text read silently for testing purposes are often read aloud later. In the discussion that follows, comprehension can be reexamined or deepened, keeping 'critical reading' in mind, especially in the upper classes. It is important that the pupil realizes that he is not practising speed but rather the techniques of reading, which can only be mastered through a great deal of practice. More important than technical exercises is reading itself and the child's self-confidence. The best encouragement comes about when the pupil sees for himself that his test results have improved, and that his progress is affected by the number of books he reads. This he comes to appreciate from his reader passport where the names of the books are entered. The value to the child of a record of the test results should, however, not be underestimated. It offers constant proof of the child's achievement, raising his self-confidence and, at the same time, challenging him to further achievement. A glance at the entries shows him where he once stood and how far he has come in the meantime. In the upper classes the numerical results of the tests will become meaningless for skilled children, as they reach a point where they can apparently no longer improve; however, the survey of books read will express the volume of their reading and will show them how much they have gained. They will appreciate that they have developed personal preferences; in short they have become 'readers'.

However important it is that the pupil be able to choose his own books, it is just as important that the teacher recognizes the needs and interests of the child and helps him in the selection of reading matter. This is why the reader passport has two pages with book recommendations in conjunction with the scores for reading achievement. With many children the readability of a text, that is the level of difficulty, plays a more important role than reading interests. The essential finding of a study using the reader passport is the importance of practice in improving the standard of reading. Still more interesting is the parallel between progress in reading and the number of books read during a given period; but it is difficult to portray this in a few examples. When we examined the cases where children read well, we found that at school they had not only acquired the ability to read, but books had also been in the foreground from the very beginning. Thus the paradoxical sequel: Many children do not read books because they cannot read; they cannot read because they do not read books.

This insight brought about a fundamental change in our method of bringing children and books together. Whereas we had previously begun our work with the book—to find the right book and make it available—the child himself now became the starting point. That is effective reading education with the help of genuine children's books. As reading children's books has turned out to be the best aid to the teaching of reading, different ways of luring children into reading have been considered (Bamberger 1972).

It is important to consider also the role of the librarian in bridging the gap between reading people and children's book people. What can the librarian do to help? First of all, the librarian will try not only to serve his reader but also to win new readers. He cannot be satisfied with the fact that he brings the best books to the best readers (that is, to about 30 or 40 per cent of the children), but he will ask himself how he can help the beginning readers and the backward readers. There are many ways, but surely one of the best is to help the teacher by supplying her with those books she needs to lure the whole class or groups of readers into reading. The librarian will have collections of simplified texts for the backward readers and will also try to find books of literary quality which are easy to read. If he lets teachers and parents know about these endeavours they will feel that they are receiving assistance in their difficult task. Of course, the noble aim of distributing the best books among the children will remain, but it is not enough just to offer these books; the librarian needs the teacher and perhaps also a device like a reader passport to reach a wider range of children.

The important need, for the moment, is for teachers and children's book people to begin to realize more clearly that they need each other, that they have to try to bridge the gap between themselves. This is not just a pious wish, but a task for the professional organizations of both sides. This is why we in Austria have changed the name and the function of our International Institute for Children's Literature to International Institute for Children's Literature and Reading Research. This is why professional organizations of both groups should invite speakers and participants from the other side to conferences and discussions. More use should be made of mutually available materials, publications and advertising. Both groups should perhaps cooperate in convincing public opinion so that they will both receive more financial assistance. This cooperation is especially important in view of the dangers that the new technical media—especially television—have for reading education. The *book* will always be able to enter into competition or to cooperate with new media. The danger lies in the fact that many children do not find the time to read the number of books necessary to make them readers in the true sense of the word. The chief aim of cooperation between the reading people and the children's book people is not just to raise reading standards. The main aim is, and will remain, to help young people to find joy and fulfilment in reading throughout their lives.

## References

BAMBERGER, R. (1966) Lure into reading *Bookbird 4* Vienna: International Institute for Children's Literature and Reading Research

BAMBERGER, R. (1968) Measuring and increasing reading ability *Bookbird 2* Vienna: International Institute for Children's Literature and Reading Research

BAMBERGER, R. (1970) *Reading and Children's Books* Vienna: International Institute for Children's Juvenile and Popular Literature

BAMBERGER, R. (1971) *Lese-Erziehung* (Reading Education) Vienna: International Institute for Children's Literature and Reading Research

BAMBERGER, R. (1972a) The reader passport *Bookbird 1* Vienna: International Institute for Children's Literature and Reading Research

BAMBERGER, R. (1972b) Developing lifelong reading interests and reading habits *Bookbird 2* Vienna: International Institute for Children's Literature and Reading Research

BAMBERGER, R. (1972c) 'International activities to promote children's reading and children's literature (with special reference to central Europe)' in V. Southgate (ed) *Literacy at all Levels* London: Ward Lock Educational

BAMBERGER, R. (no date) *Jugendschriftenkunde* (Study of Children's Books) Vienna: International Institute for Children's Juvenile and Popular Literature

MORRIS, J. M. (1966) *Standards and Progress in Reading* Slough: National Foundation for Educational Research

# Part four Related skills


## *11  Further thoughts on spelling: caught or taught?*

Margaret L. Peters


### Introduction

In this paper the intention is three-fold:

1  To indicate the difficulties of learning to spell as opposed to learning to read, difficulties which stem from the nature of the skill itself, and from the very nature of the English language.
2  To consider these difficulties which tend to confront if not overwhelm the linguistically ill-favoured child but which are surmountable in school.
3  To argue that these do not constitute a case for a radical change in spelling, which might well be a facilitating device in the initial teaching of literacy but a dangerously divisive tool socially.

### *Difficulties of learning to spell as opposed to learning to read*

#### Differences in the two skills

Spelling skill is not only a poor but a very distant relation of reading skill. It is poor in that its place in the school curriculum is ill-defined. Often indeed 'the traditional spelling lesson is an ad hoc approach to the task of internalization and one which for lack of awareness of the orthography falls back on random procedures and on rote-learning' (Mackay *et al* 1970). It is distant because of the nature of the skill itself which makes learning to spell a very different matter from learning to read since reading is a decoding and spelling an encoding process. This can be put another way. In reading, discriminatory skills coincide with understanding, but emphasis on these is reduced until the competent reader not only does not fixate letters, but not even words and there is no conscious awareness of component units. In spelling, understanding a word or phrase necessarily precedes writing it. And before the automatic, predictable, infallible spelling of which Schonell spoke is achieved, there may be a conscious deliberation in selection of the correct alternative, a predetermined strategy, followed necessarily by much writing practice.

It is a useful exercise to contrast yet further these two skills, the two RS whose reflection of linguistic competence is interdependent yet so dissimilar. In the first place reading skill is flexible. Considerable variance is possible in performance, depending on the purpose for which one is reading, but in spelling such variance is not acceptable, for spelling does not vary according to the occasion, except in so far as shorthand takes the place of longhand when a secretary receives dictation! Secondly, reading permits successive approximations to the word being read, before commitment, while in spelling, once one has committed oneself on paper, there is no going back. Again, learning to read entails a fanning upward of success due to environmental reinforcement even after a child has left school. Such a child has little reason or inclination to write, and the reluctant writer has little reinforcement of spelling success, since writing is by no means as pervasive an activity as reading. Finally, skill in reading is progressive in the sense that it improves year by year with experience and practice. Spelling on the other hand is much more an all or none activity according to the individual's approach, his perceptual habits, his imagery, his attitudes, casual or careful, and most of all his self-image.

## Difficulties in the two skills

But there is a difference between the two skills which stems from the nature of the English language itself. Various estimates (Groff 1961, Hildreth 1956, Venezky and Lester 1964) put the percentage of English words that are graphophonemically regular at about 80 per cent. Now in reading the problem (if children have acquired a phonic system which by definition operates for 80 per cent of the language), is only with the 20 per cent of so-called irregular words.

In spelling there is not only difficulty with this 20 per cent of *irregular* words (*that* is only to be expected) but with the 80 per cent of graphophonemically *regular* words that could have quite reasonable alternatives, 'train' could reasonably be written 'trane', or 'certain' 'surten'—and as long as we cling to the *sound* of the word we are relying on a precarious strategy since each sound can be encoded in various quite reasonable forms.

## The nature of the spelling skill

As humans sight is our preferred sense: we rely on looking to check our uncertainties in spelling. We implicitly associate structurally similar words. This is because the probability of words conforming to spelling precedent is very high, and it is by becoming familiar with spelling precedents that we become good spellers. In other words familiarity with a coding system is half the battle in learning to spell.

To be able to spell is to have learned a coding system based on the probabilities of letters occurring in certain sequences. Wallach (1963) presented good and poor spellers with briefly exposed flash cards bearing nonsense words in random letter sequence e.g. dnehps, or nonsense words that are a close approximation to English e.g. aphyst or epidol. He found that though there was very little difference between good and poor spellers in random letter sequences, the good spellers were found to recognize nonsense words resembling English much more readily than poor spellers. The good spellers had acquired generalizing ability. What they wrote was in line with spelling precedent in English. Now this competence is language-specific; Bruner and Harcourt (1953) demonstrated this by presenting nonsense words to the members of an international seminar, but the nonsense words were words like mjolkkor, epilaterre, fattaloni and delegates found no difficulty in reproducing words that were nonsense in their own language as against 'foreign' languages. As Bruner says: 'When one learns a language one learns a coding system that goes beyond words.' And once one has acquired the code one can spell. This is why spelling can be said to be an all or none activity. The spelling of a child who has acquired the code is not inevitably (nor should one pedantically insist on its being) correct on all occasions, but errors when they do occur are reasonable phonic alternatives, i.e. alternatives according to spelling precedent, and as such communication is not unduly affected (at least no more than that the reader notes that an error has occurred and is momentarily diverted from the content of the communication).

Prediction of disability more informative than testing

The all or none nature of spelling suggests the importance of the prediction of spelling disability in the individual child as opposed to conventional testing. There is evidence (Peters 1970) that to know certain things about a child makes it possible to predict that he is at risk with spelling and to take preventive measures. Since spelling is not progressive, as is reading, we are not concerned normatively with whether a child has a 'spelling age' somewhere near his chronological age, but where he comes on a continuum such as: careless, casual, adequate, careful, pedantic, and whether his visual perception of word form is good, that is how he looks at words, sees, and reproduces them, for this is within the scope of poor spellers if they try. Unfortunately so often they have just never challenged themselves or been challenged to make the attempt.

*Difficulties confronting some children*

Which children catch spelling?

These attributes are clearly ones that, like spelling ability as a whole, are caught within that network of linguistic constraints that is the privilege of linguistically advantaged children. For what most strongly influences spelling ability is verbal intelligence. It is only to be expected that the younger the child the more the home environment affects spelling ability. By home environment is meant not only socioeconomic status, but whether a child is an eldest or only child rather than a middle or youngest, and whether he comes from a small rather than a larger family. But by the time the child is eleven, his spelling ability is determined more by the teaching which he has experienced than by his home background. And then it is what the teacher does, most particularly in those who begin at a low attainment level, that matters.

Children who don't catch spelling—the responsibility of the teacher
The conditions necessary for the effective teaching of such children are laid bare in the research reported in *Success in Spelling* (Peters 1970). It is quite clear from the evidence that progress in spelling occurs when teachers' attitudes are consistent and when they themselves are rational and systematic in their teaching. In the survey of one LEA age group when classes were ranked for mean percentage spelling progress none of the classes in the top half had a really inconsistent irrational and unsystematic teacher, and no classes in the bottom half had a thoroughly systematic and rational teacher.

One of the questions that most concerns teachers is whether children learn to spell best by learning from lists, and if so what kind of lists. The evidence is clear. They do learn best by lists but only if the lists are of words derived from their own needs (i.e. either words which the children ask for in the course of their free writing or lists drawn up by the teacher from the kind of words the children ask for). Then there is significantly greater progress than if printed lists or no lists at all are used (see Clark pp. 11–12).

Such 'individual asked for' and 'teacher-prepared' lists of words must, of course, be learned and tested, regularly and systematically, a tall order for any teacher of a large class. In such a situation the onus must be on the child (see Reid p. 30). He must, as Arvidson says, 'be encouraged to adopt a particularly determined attitude towards words that persistently give him trouble', and Arvidson's (1964) technique of indicating to each child the 'frequency' of the word he is learning, and relating it to the frequency level a child of his age should be working at, puts the responsibility for learning and testing himself in the child's hands. Another way of encouraging active self-testing is for the child to test himself by looking at the word to be learned, covering it up and writing it as a whole (without blindly copying), checking and repeating the procedure till he can write the word correctly without reference (Peters 1967). An economical practice examined by Bernard *et al* (1931) quoted in the *Scottish Studies in Spelling* (1961) is the test-study as opposed to the conventional study-test method. Here, for example, children working in pairs test each other first and omit those words in the list that are correct before learning those that are incorrect.

Now another area of spelling teaching which is crucial is how teachers expect children to 'do corrections'. Some demand that children should 'write out each mistake three times'; others expect correction sequences e.g. the children finding their own mistakes, looking them up and writing them from memory. The difference in the progress of classes with rote as distinct from rational correction techniques is very marked. Again the onus is on the child in actively learning the words with which he has failed.

Perhaps the most vital contribution to spelling that a teacher can make from the very beginning is the teaching of handwriting. This must be swift and effortless, yet well formed. It was surprising in the survey to find that those children who wrote swiftly also wrote carefully; it is a myth that swift writers write carelessly. The swifter the writing the better the spelling. This is only to be expected, since the child that writes swiftly is accustomed to writing familiar strings of letters together and, as we have seen, there is a high probability of certain strings occurring and recurring in English. Swift writing reveals confidence and engenders competence, and the swift writer who sees himself as a good speller *is* a good speller for spelling, as we have seen, is, unlike reading, an all or none activity, and it is crucial that the child who is linguistically ill-favoured should be given in school, by systematic, rational teaching the power of written communication that is his right.

*Is there a case for a radical change in spelling?*
That spelling *can* be taught to less verbally intelligent children is indisputable; the question is *should it*? Does our orthography (in which about one in five words is graphophonemically irregular) stand up to the claims made for simplification?

Practical considerations
A strong case for a simplified spelling system has indeed been made not only in the Scandinavian but in European countries and has been implemented. The case has been argued extensively (Poll 1972). The situation in English is different. In the first instance English orthography has, to quote Mackay *et al* (1970), been 'petrified'. This is a strong word in the light of the subtle changing of our spelling system over the centuries. Yet in attributing this petrification to universal literacy, recalling the 'millions of people whose internalized mastery of spelling has become deeply embedded in their mental processes', there seems to be implied a stabilizing of our spelling system. Presumably the millions would resist a radical change in the spelling system, a change that

would dwarf to sober proportions any problems of decimalization and metrication. It is not that printing presses could not cope with the *new* tide of literature—but could they reproduce the great sea of printed texts already in print? A new spelling system would, when learned, allow for a generation or two, access to the literature of the past, but there are grave dangers that in a hundred years 'prespelling change literature' might like Gothic script or Chaucerian verse become a minority privilege.

### Sociological considerations

Again it has to be remembered that English is almost a universal language on both sides of the Atlantic and presumably the sun never sets on places where English is spoken if not as a first then as a second language. Now with the anticipation of universal literacy in developing countries one can speculate about the justice of changing a spelling system and depriving the newly literate of the literature of the past. A simplified alphabet, like basic English, would be a facilitating but diverse tool, and the responsibilities of the teacher would be even more crucial, charged as she would be not only to teach initial literacy, but to teach a second and somewhat archaic and elaborated written code if her children were to enjoy a common literary heritage.

It is possible too that the odd quirks of our orthography provide those minimal cues which make it possible for skilled readers to attain a much faster rate than they could in a graphophonemically regular writing system even though such a system unquestionably speeds and facilitates the initial learning of the reading skill. Gimson (1962) speaks of a graphophonemically regular writing system as being 'cumbersome' and continues 'our present imperfect writing system allows speed of silent reading at least twice that of speech'. Although our present writing system favours these skilled readers in facilitating their attainment of speed in reading, it unquestionably militates against the poor reader in *initial* learning to read. But a sociological problem rears itself here, for the social fact is that a change in the spelling system might accentuate the danger of minority access to our culture through the printed word. Would we, in not perpetuating our writing system, *in fact* be perpetuating an élite?

### ita—initial facilitation *with transfer*

It is a fact that our present writing system is a restrictive and not completely facile medium for the less favoured in our society. This can, as Southgate and Warburton (1969) showed, be overcome by an initial teaching medium viz, ita in which transfer to traditional orthography is inbuilt. Children who learn to read by ita are eventually completely at home in traditional orthography otherwise they would clearly be deprived of much in our culture. In the case, then, of a universally applied simplified spelling system we might well expect such deprivation, such lack of access to the culture and literature of the past, to obtain universally. Are we not in fact, by retaining our present somewhat idiosyncratic spelling system, ensuring that from our literary heritage 'magic casements' remain open for all?

Literary speculations!
There is always in addition the intriguing speculation that a gain in precision in a simplified spelling system might be at the expense of a loss in richness, in evocation of that play on words which accompanies ambiguity. (For a scholarly exploration of syntactic and semantic ambiguities see Empson 1947.) Is there something in those quirks of our writing system which enliven not only what but *how* to write? Does Lady Macbeth's intention to 'gild the faces of the grooms withall/For it may seem their guilt' seem just that bit more pungent to twentieth century eyes because of the spelling of that sinister play on words? At least the ambiguity is patent and not restricted to an intellectual élite as it might be in a simplified alphabet offering 'gild' and 'gilt'.

It has been shown that to retain our present spelling system is to keep open the flood-gates of literature. This being so, to ensure that we maintain our literary tradition, it is important to provide children with the necessary medium.

*The medium and the message*
Many teachers are content to ignore spelling and similar constraints provided that the writing is vivid and exciting. Yet it is only when we have achieved that machine-like spelling of which Schonell spoke that we are really free to write with confidence, with no backward glances to see if a word 'looks right', and with no offering of a less precise synonym or phrase because the right one is difficult to spell. The competent and hence confident speller will explore new ways of expressing himself. He will experiment with new words, which up till now may have been passive. The new words tentatively tried out in conversation are becoming active. For the competent and confident speller these words will become active on paper for he, accustomed to the likelihood of certain sequences of letters in English, will, from his experience in handling such sequences, make a confident and fairly accurate attempt. But the poor speller may avoid using the new and exciting word. He may use a simpler and less precise circumlocution. He may not write at all.

Far from being freed to write creatively by ignoring spelling and similar conventions, some children, and adults, are only freed to write when they have learnt to spell correctly. It is like a pianist who can only interpret the music when he knows it 'by heart'. Only when he has reached the stage of muscular recall, and no longer has to go via the medium of visual recognition, only when he is unworried by the intricacies of the written score or by the technicalities of fingering, and the fingers move in sequence, can he attend not to the symbols but to the sound that emerges. In the same way the writer, unworried by the intricacies of spelling, can write as freely as he can speak, can expand his ideas, can give examples, figures of speech, confidently and adventurously.

This sort of freedom in writing is a necessary condition not only of academic education, but of written communication in any form. As long as we continue to communicate in *writing* and not electronically whether in correspondence, in prose, in poetry, or in scientific records, the message is permanent and can be reread, reconsidered and amended selectively and at a self-chosen speed. This is not the case with the message on magnetic tape which is not only transitory in 'playback' but is transmitted aurally. And if, as I have argued, vision is our preferred sense, recording the message on magnetic tape is in a very much less favoured and less satisfactory modality.

For it is after all the message that counts, but only in so far as the message can not only be received and remain available, but can also be transmitted, since without the medium there can clearly be no message.

*References*

ARVIDSON, G. L. (1964) *Learning to Spell* Oxford: Wheaton

BERNARD, A. M. (1931) An experimental study in spelling *Supplement to Scottish Education Journal* 5, June 1931, described in Scottish Council for Research in Education (1962) *Studies in Spelling* London: University of London Press

BRUNER, J. S. and HARCOURT, R. A. F. (1953) *Going Beyond the Information Given* unpublished manuscript

EMPSON, W. (1947) *Seven Types of Ambiguity* London: Chatto and Windus

GIMSON, C. A. (1962) 'The transmission of English' in R. Quirk (ed) *The Use of English* London: Longman

GROFF, P. J. (1961) The new Iowa spelling scale: how phonetic is it? *Elementary School Journal* 9, 2, 46–49

HILDRETH, G. M. (1956) *Teaching Spelling* New York: Henry Holt

MACKAY, D., THOMPSON, B. and SCHAUB, P. (1970) *Breakthrough to Literacy Teachers' Manual* London: Longman

PETERS, M. L. (1967) *Spelling: Caught or Taught?* London: Routledge and Kegan Paul

PETERS, M. L. (1970) *Success in Spelling* Cambridge: Cambridge Institute of Education

POLL, L. K. (1972) Een Spellingsreis *Cultural Supplement* Uitgave Van NRC Handelsblad 85

SCHONELL, F. J. (1942) *Backwardness in the Basic Subjects* Edinburgh: Oliver and Boyd

SOUTHGATE, V. and WARBURTON, F. W. (1-969) *ita.: an Independent Evaluation* London: John Murray/Edinburgh: W. & R. Chambers

WALLACH, M. A. (1963) Perceptual recognition of approximations to English in relation to spelling achievement *Journal of Educational Psychology* 54, 1, 57–62

## 12  How to teach reading by the aid of Regularized Inglish

*Axel M. Wijk*

I will begin with two short anecdotes which I think have a very close bearing on my subject. From 1948 to 1951 I held a temporary appointment as lecturer in Swedish at Columbia University in New York City. My wife and my two small children then aged four and two had come with me to New York where we got an apartment quite close to the university. We at once put our children in a playschool and in much less than a year they spoke English like the other children of the same age.

At the beginning of our third year we put our son, who was then six years old, into the local public school (public in the American sense). In the playschool there had been no attempt whatever to teach him to read and write. In the first grade, our son read only three booklets: *We look and see*, *We come and go* and *We work and play*. These booklets consisted mainly of pictures with texts underneath and they contained in all, fifty-eight different words which were repeated over and over again, scores of times, until they were learnt by heart, but without any reference to the connection between individual letters and sounds. They were thus based on the pure so-called 'whole word' method.

One day, probably towards the end of the second term, my son came home from school very proud because the teacher had taught them the word 'gun', which she had put on the blackboard. All American boys of that age take a keen interest in everything connected with cowboys and cowboy equipment. Then I suddenly got the idea that I'd have some fun with my son, so I told him that I was going to change the word 'gun' a little to see whether he could then read it. Now his name happens to be Gunnar, which is a very common name in Sweden. By that time he had probably seen his name written a good many times. I now added the last three letters of his name to the word 'gun' and then asked him if he could read it. He stared hard at it for a while and then—he was quite a bright little chap—he exclaimed: 'Holster, holster!'

Well, that's the whole-word method for you in a nutshell. It's sheer guessing! It has nothing whatever to do with real reading. Those of you who have read Flesch's (1955) well-known book, *Why Johnny Can't Read*, will surely remember the little boy who could always read the word 'chicken' when it was shown to him on a flash card, but who could never read or recognize it when he came across it in a printed sentence. And when the teacher at last asked him how it was that he was able to read the word when he saw it on the flash card, he answered: 'Well, there is a little smudge in the upper right-hand corner.'

I might perhaps add here that when we returned to Sweden after our three years in America, our daughter, who did not know any Swedish at all at that time, didn't start going to the regular school till two years later, when she was seven years old. During her first year at school her class, which was taught according to the phonic method, read only one book but this contained about 125 full pages of text and nearly 1,900 different words. As a rule we never bother to count the number of words that the children learn, for once they have learnt the rules of pronunciation of our spelling system, they should be able to read any word that they come across in books that are intended for their age level.

The first thing we can learn from these little anecdotes is that memorizing words as wholes cannot, properly speaking, be called reading at all. What then exactly is real reading? Since I am a linguist and to some extent also a phonetician, I would like to define it from their standpoint in the first place. Real reading consists in the continuous translation of written or printed symbols into the corresponding spoken sounds, in doing which it is essential to proceed from left to right, anyway when we have to do with European languages and not for example with Chinese. Whether the words are spoken out aloud or not is of no consequence, since the spoken form is obviously the primary one, as appears from the fact that it was in existence first and that writing was invented in order to render the spoken language. When one 'reads' a word as a whole, one takes in its total configuration at one glance, so to speak, and it is of no importance if one starts from the beginning or the end, and there is no question of observing the separate sounds of which the word is made up. A child may then recognize a word by some special, actually quite irrelevant peculiarity; for instance 'aeroplane' by its unusual length or 'monkey' by its 'tail', the y at the end etc.

Somebody might ask whether it is essential to understand what you read in order to call it real reading. From the linguist's and the phonetician's point of view I would say no, *primarily* that is not in the essence of reading. If for example you have learnt the rules of pronunciation for French or German, you will be able to read, i.e. to pronounce, lots of printed French or German words which you may not understand, because you have not as yet learnt their meaning. Similarly, we can read texts in our own language, which we do not understand, because they are too technical or in other ways beyond our level of knowledge or experience. But that does not by itself mean that we are unable to read. Usually, however, we only read about things that we are more or less familiar with and which we have therefore no difficulty in understanding. We might recall in this connection that in phonetic exercises it is very common to practice reading nonsense words and to dictate nonsense words to the students, which they must then write down in order to show that they are able to perceive and distinguish the various speech sounds correctly.

To prevent misunderstanding I should perhaps add here that when I say that understanding the meaning of what one reads is not *primarily* in the essence of reading, I do not mean that *reading in its full sense* consists merely in being able to pronounce or decode various individual printed or written words. But that is the goal that we must try to attain in the first place, when we want to teach children to read, because only in this way can we provide a safe and reliable key to the decoding of all words. As we work our way towards this goal, we may gradually proceed to the subsequent stages in the development of the ability to read: the comprehension of both simple and more or less complicated sentences and the comprehension of connected stories and of more or less involved ideas and arguments.

If we then turn more specifically to the problem of teaching reading, I would first emphasize that there are two sides to the question, which are not always kept strictly apart. On the one hand, there is the primary problem of teaching children to read, and on the other, there is the secondary problem of teaching them to write or spell correctly. From the point of view of the native speaker, this latter aspect of the problem easily becomes the predominant one, as is indicated by the names of the societies which have been founded to work for an improvement in the ability to read and write—the British and the American Simplified *Spelling*, not simplified *Reading*, Societies. Nevertheless the other aspect of the problem, that of making it easier to learn to read, is actually far more important, because until you have learnt to read, there can be no question of learning to spell correctly.

It is a well-established fact that the teaching of reading presents exceptional difficulties in the English-speaking countries and that this is mainly due to the orthographical system of the language, which is extremely antiquated and confused. According to official investigations into reading ability in Great Britain, more than a quarter of the nation's children must still at the age of fifteen be classified as backward readers. Very similar conditions obtain in America, as may be seen for example from Flesch's *Why Johnny Can't Read*, which became a best-seller, evidently because so many parents had found that their children had great difficulties in learning to read.

The chief explanation of this deplorable state of affairs is undoubtedly the fact that owing to the large number of irregular spellings among the commonest words in the language, it is not possible to lay down any rules for the connection between spelling and pronunciation that would be useful to children who are beginning to learn to read. Most of the reading schemes that are in general use therefore prefer, to begin with, to employ the so-called whole-word method, which aims at teaching children each regularly or irregularly written word as a whole, without paying much attention to the pronunciation of the individual letters. When the children have acquired a not too small basic vocabulary of look-and-say or sight words, they are gradually introduced to the so-called phonic method, i.e. the old time-honoured method of sounding out the various letters and combinations of letters. Since this method can only be applied to certain categories of words, it will still be necessary to continue employing the look-and-say method for a considerable number of words which belong to the commonest in the language. Owing to this mixture of methods it is hardly to be wondered at if children should get the general impression that there are no reliable rules concerning the relationship between spelling and pronunciation in their language.

In spite of the impression of irregularity and confusion that the English language is bound to make on the young beginner, its pronunciation and spelling are not nearly so confused as most people are apt to think. When we come to examine its entire vocabulary, we shall indeed find that this impression is very largely wrong and that the vast majority of English words, about 90 to 95 per cent of the vocabulary, actually follow certain general rules or patterns, whereas only 5 to 10 per cent display definitely irregular spellings. It is only among the commonest words that we find an exceptionally high percentage of irregular words, amounting to between 20 and 30 per cent. Since the 3,000 commonest words, as given in Thorndike and Lorge (1944), usually cover about 95 per cent of the running words on an average page of prose Bongers (1947), it is not surprising if one is often misled into believing that English spelling is far more irregular than it actually is.

If we now revert to the question of teaching reading it must, quite obviously, be an extremely exacting task for little children of from five to six or seven years of age to learn to master the various rules of the complicated English spelling system, if at the same time they have to learn a large number of exceptions to the rules of the system. If we want to make it easier for children to learn to read, the most rational and very likely also the simplest and most efficient way of achieving this, is to change these irregular spellings into regular ones for the period during which children are learning to read, and thus make it possible for them to concentrate on mastering the regular phonic units of the spelling system before attempting to learn the numerous exceptions to it. This is what has been done in *Regularized Inglish*, apart from certain minor modifications in the spelling system. By way of illustration I will supply the following list of examples of irregular spellings in the existing orthography which have been replaced by regular ones in this *temporarily modified or 'reformed' system of spelling.*

G

| Traditional orthography | Regularized Inglish |
| --- | --- |
| any, many, said, says, quay, | eny, meny, sed, sez, kea, |
| calf, half, calm, aunt, laugh, | caaf, haaf, caam, aant, laaf, |
| false, salt, talk, walk, water, | faulse, sault, tauk, wauk, wauter, |
| all, ball, call, fall, small, | aull, baull, caull, faull, smaull, |
| also, almost, already, although, | aulso, aulmoste, aulreddy, aultho, |
| want, wash, watch, was, what, | wont, wosh, wotch, woz, whot, |
| war, warm, quarter, quarrel, | waur, waurm, quaurter, quorrel, |
| are, scarcely. | ar, scaircely. |
| | |
| bread, head, ready, steady, | bred, hed, reddy, steddy, |
| health, feather, pleasant, meadow, | helth, fether, plezant, meddoe, |
| heaven, heavy, sweater, weapon, | heven, hevy, swetter, weppon, |
| great, break, bear, tear, wear, | greit, breik, bair, tair, wair, |
| early, learn, heard, heart, height, | erly, lern, herd, hart, hight, |
| clerk, there, where, were, | clark, thare, whare, wer, |
| England, English, pretty. | Ingland, Inglish, pritty. |
| | |
| eye, key, receive, seize, people, | ie, kee, receev, seeze, peeple, |
| have, give, live, gone, shone, | hav, giv, liv, gon, shon, |
| machine, police, climb, friend. | mashien, poliece, clime, frend. |
| | |
| do, who, lose, woman, women, | doo, hoo, looze, woomman, wimmen, |
| colour, cover, come, some, among, | cullour, cuver, cum, sum, amung, |
| done, none, son, one, once, onion, | dun, nun, sun, wun, wunce, unnion, |
| | |
| money, month, mother, other, | munney, munth, muther, uther, |
| nothing, | nuthing, |
| love, above, move, prove, dozen | luv, abuv, moov, proov, duzzen, |
| word, work, world, worm, worth, | wurd, wurk, wurld, wurm, wurth, |
| borough, thorough, worry. | burro, thurro, wurry. |
| | |
| broad, does, shoe, blood, flood, | braud, duz, shoo, blud, flud, |
| double, trouble, couple, country, | dubble, trubble, cupple, cuntry, |
| enough, rough, tough, cough, | enuff, ruff, tuff, coff, |
| dough, though, through | do, tho, thru, |
| bought, brought, fought, ought, | baught, braught, faught, aught, |
| could, should, would, shoulder, | cood, shood, wood, shoelder, |
| you, your, youth, young. | yoo, yoor, yooth, yung. |
| | |
| blow, grow, know, low, own, | bloe, groe, knoe, loe, oen, |
| only, don't, won't, | oenly, doen't, woen't, |
| roll, stroll, folk, yolk, | roell, stroell, foek, yoek, |
| course, four, pour, journal, journey, | corse, foar, poar, jurnal, jurney, |
| courage, flourish, nourish, | currage, flurrish, nurrish, |

| | |
|---|---|
| full, pull, bush, push, put, | fooll, pooll, boosh, poosh, poot, |
| bury, busy, business, build. | bery, bizzy, bizness, bild. |
| | |
| debt, doubt, lamb, bomb, comb, | det, dout, lam, bom, coem, |
| honest, honour, hour, heir, | onnest, onnour, our, eir, |
| island, almond, salmon, autumn, | iland, aamond, sammon, autum, |
| of, castle, listen, whistle, | ov, caasle, lissen, whissle, |
| sugar, sure, answer, two, whole. | shugar, shure, aanser, too, hoel. |

It is a well-known fact that the orthographical system of the English language is extremely antiquated and confused. Many attempts have therefore been made in the past to devise a suitable new system of spelling for the language. The solution that most immediately presents itself is to create a new phonetic alphabet for English by selecting the most suitable symbol for each of its forty odd speech sounds. These symbols are then to be used as consistently as possible for the spelling of all words. Among the best and most carefully thought out systems of this kind undoubtedly is the one devised by the British Simplified Spelling Society, who in 1940 brought out their publication, *New Spelling*, based on a careful statistical investigation of the present spelling. In order to create a more phonetic spelling the Simplified Spelling Society introduced special new symbols for the so-called long sounds of the five simple vowels, namely *ae, ee, ie, oe* and *ue*. These symbols were to be used in all words in which the speech sounds in question are found, whether now represented by the simple vowel letters or by combinations of vowel letters or by combinations of vowel letters with certain consonants. In view of the frequent occurrence of these sounds it is obvious that this feature was bound to cause an extremely violent break in continuity between the traditional and the suggested new system of spelling. Other features of the Simplified Spelling Society's *New Spelling* which would contribute to causing similar violent breaks in continuity were the regular replacing of c and q by k, when they stood for the k sound, of c by s, whenever it stood for the voiceless s sound, and of g by j, when it represented the regular j sound. The effect of the proposed changes in spelling was such as to cause a complete transformation in the appearance of the language. There is nothing very wrong with the system as such, but when we come to examine it more closely, we shall find that it leads to a change in spelling in 90 per cent or more of the vocabulary. It is not surprising therefore that it never succeeded in arousing any widespread interest among either teachers or the general public.

Since the phonetic principle leads to such extensive changes in the spelling, and since a solution of this kind obviously does not stand the slightest chance of ever being accepted, we shall have to examine whether there may not be other methods of achieving a systematic reform. The only alternative that offers the possibility of *a general revision* of the whole spelling system is to start out instead from the various existing symbols and try to determine how they should best be used in a reformed orthography. What we have to do exactly, is first to examine in detail how these symbols are now used, and then to decide which uses may conveniently be retained and which should be discarded. Generally speaking, all the regular, i.e. the most frequent uses of the various sound symbols, should be preserved, whereas all irregular spellings should be discarded and replaced by regular ones. If in the application of these general rules we give up the idea of strict adherence to the phonetic principle and allow, on the one hand, certain symbols to represent more than one sound and, on the other, certain sounds to be represented by more than one symbol, when this can be done without causing undue confusion, we shall find that it becomes possible to work out a spelling system for English which on the whole may be said to satisfy all reasonable requirements with regard to order and regularity and which will enable us to establish definite rules of pronunciation for the English language. Since the fundamental idea of this 'new' system of spelling is to preserve *all* the various sound symbols of the present orthography in their *regular*, i.e. in their most frequent usage or usages, it may suitably be called Regularized Inglish. On a closer examination it will be found that the principles of Regularized Inglish enable us to retain the present spelling in over 90 per cent of the vocabulary, whereas the new spelling of the Simplified Spelling Society only preserves it in 10 per cent or less.

I have referred to Regularized Inglish as a new system of spelling for English and the impression may have been conveyed that I am proposing that the spelling of English should be reformed right away. Even though I am convinced that a sensible spelling reform would offer the most rational solution to the reading problem, I cherish no illusions as to the possibility of bringing about such a reform within the immediately foreseeable future. That is a long-term project on which the English-speaking peoples will evidently have to make up their own minds. All I am suggesting for the time being is therefore that we should introduce regularized Inglish as a transitional spelling system which will make it considerably easier for English-speaking children to learn to read and write. By the aid of regularized Inglish ordinary English may be turned into a phonetic language or rather into a language with a *regular* spelling system which can be taught in accordance with definite rules of pronunciation in much the same way as this is now being done in the case of other phonetic languages, such as German, Italian, Spanish or Swedish. Once the children have learnt to master the rules of this spelling system, they should be able to read any not too unusual word that they come across, and there will no longer be any need for learning new words by heart or for keeping records of the number of words that they have learnt to recognize. It should be emphasized that *Regularized Inglish is not really a new system of spelling for English.* Except for certain not very extensive modifications, it is nothing but the regular system of spelling that is inherent in ordinary English and which emerges when we eliminate the 5 to 10 per cent of irregular spellings in the language and replace them by regular ones.

It should further be noted that as soon as children have learnt to read Regularized Inglish, which for children of normal ability who begin to receive more formal instruction in reading at about six years of age, will probably take about a year or so, they will immediately be able to read English in the traditional orthography as well, in spite of the many irregularities of spelling, for once they have learnt to read according to one system of spelling, there is no great difficulty about reading according to another which employs the same characters. Thus, for example, all foreign children who have learnt to read their own language and who belong to nations using the Roman alphabet, will be able to read most English words at first sight, though of course without the proper pronunciation and without understanding them. When children have finally learnt to read with ease texts written in Regularized Inglish, the time will have come for them to learn also to write correctly, in accordance with the spelling of ordinary English. Knowing how to read is the key to learning about everything else, even about learning to spell correctly.

In my discussion of Regularized Inglish I have only been able to describe the general principles which characterize this spelling system. For a detailed account of the rules of pronunciation for the various symbols that are used to render the forty-six speech sounds of which English is made up, see Wijk 1959, 1960, 1966a, 1966b, 1971.

The essential advantage of the regularized system of spelling that I have proposed, is that it restores to the language an intimate relationship between spelling and pronunciation, while at the same time it preserves all the characteristic regular features of the present spelling system. It enables us to lay down definite rules of pronunciation for the various letters and combinations of letters which on the whole will prove entirely adequate. Naturally the rules are not quite so simple as in a more completely phonetic system of orthography, but they are not very complicated either, and above all they will make it possible for all native speakers to acquire the ability to read English by means of systematic study of the rules of pronunciation for the various existing sound symbols. This being so, it need hardly be emphasized what important consequences the general adoption of this new medium would have for the improvement of the ability to read and write in the English-speaking countries.

*Two brief specimens of Regularized Inglish*
The extracts are taken from *Alphabets for English* (Haas 1969).

Objections to a chainge in the prezent spelling
We instinctivly shrink from eny chainge in whot iz familiar; and
whot can be more familiar than the form ov wurds that we hav
seen and written more times than we can possibly estimate? We
take up a book printed in America, and 'honor' and 'center' jar
upon us every time we cum across them; nay, even to see 'forever'
in place ov 'for ever' attracts our attention in an unpleazant way.
But theze ar isolated cases; think ov the meny wurds that wood
hav to be chainged if eny real improovment wer to rezult. At the
first glaance a passage in eny reformed spelling looks queer and
ugly. This objection iz aulwayz the first to be made; it iz perfectly
natural; it iz the hardest to remoov. Indeed, its effect iz not
weakened until the new spelling iz no longer new, until it haz been
seen offen enuff to be familiar.

By the adoption ov such a system ov spelling az Regularized
Inglish it would be possible to lay down definit rules ov pronunciation for the Inglish language, which wood make it considerably
eazier for children to lern to read and write. In aull probability it
wood lead to a saving ov at least wun year's wurk for aull scool-
children. It wood aulso contribute very largely towaurdz abolition
ov the existing amount ov illiteracy and backwardness in reading.
Finally it wood remoov the principal obstacle that prevents Inglish
from becumming a truly international language.

*References*
BONGERS, H. (1947) *History and Principles of Vocabulary Control as it
affects the Teaching of Foreign Languages in General and of English
in Particular* Woerden (Holland): Wocopi
FLESCH, R. (1955) *Why Johnny Can't Read* New York: Harper and
Row
HAAS, W. (1969) *Alphabets for English* Manchester: Manchester
University Press
THORNDIKE, E. L. (1944) *Teacher's Word Book of 30,000 Words* New
York: Bureau of Publications, Teachers' College, Columbia University
WIJK, A. (1937) *The Orthography and Pronunciation of Henry Machyn,
the London Diarist: A Study of the South-East Yorkshire Dialect in
the Early 16th Century* Doctoral dissertation at the University of
Stockholm
WIJK, A. (1959) Regularized Inglish: An investigation into the English
spelling reform problem with a new, detailed plan for a possible

solution *Acta Universitatis Stockhomiensis VII* Stockholm: Almqvist and Wiksell

WIJK, A. (1960) *The Augmented Roman Alphabet* pamphlet, Stockholm

WIJK, A. (1966) *Rules of Pronunciation for the English Language* London: Oxford University Press

WIJK, A. (1966) *Huvudreglerna for Engelskans Uttal* (The Principal Rules for the Pronunciation of English) Stockholm: Svenska Bokforlaget

WIJK, A. (1968) ita versus Regularized Inglish *Education* 88, 4, 300–312

WIJK, A. (1969) 'Regularized Inglish: the only practicable solution of the English spelling reform problem' in W. Haas (ed) *Alphabets for English* Manchester: Manchester University Press

# 13 Language prerequisites for reading

*John A. McInnes*

## Language development and reading

On the subject of the relationship of reading and language there seem to be areas of agreement among researchers and educators that promise changes and improvements in school curricula. In a synthesis of papers on language development and reading in *Reading Research Quarterly*, Irene Athey (1971) identifies some areas of agreement among the researchers represented in that volume:

> The overriding principle of agreement may be summarized in the statement that reading is not a 'skill' or even a bundle of skills, but a system of communication. This somewhat trite statement, if taken seriously, has far-reaching implications for education, because it means that reading is not viewed as a 'subject' in the curriculum, not even the subject which receives most emphasis in terms of time and resources. It is viewed as one part of the fabric of living and problem-solving which ought to be the focus of the school's efforts in organization, planning and curriculum. In this view the task of learning to read is not a matter of breaking down the reading task into a number of component skills and determining the order in which these skills should be taught. Instead it involves above all the realization that the printed word is another system of communication analogous to speech.

It has been readily observable, in North America at least, that the teaching of reading has been based to an increasing extent on the assumption that reading consists of a bundle of skills. Teaching procedures have been devised to develop particular component skills. Publishers have produced a host of materials aimed at giving pupils practice with particular skills. The testing of children's reading growth has been limited in many situations to measuring performance on certain skills. Attempts to remedy deficiencies in reading have often been based on the diagnosis of errors that supposedly reveal skill weaknesses. The skills orientation is indeed deep rooted. It would seem that if the child's reading growth is to be seen as part of his growth as a person who uses language, then present practices in teaching reading need reevaluating, modifying and in some cases dismantling.

100

The isolation of reading as a subject has become easy for schools. Periods of instruction have been set aside in which the content is reading skills. Often in these periods children have learned about reading skills much as they would learn about some other body of information. Because of the availability of many commercially produced skill-building materials, children can be put to work on tasks that are quite unrelated to the general fabric of curriculum. The materials can be handled in such a way that no connections are established to the ongoing development of thought and language in the child.

In the *New York Times*, April 1972, Joyce Maynard, an eighteen year old, looked back at school and particularly at the fragmentation of the curriculum. She reflects:

We had one fine, fancy new gimmick that followed us from fourth grade through eighth. It was a white cardboard box of folders, condensed two-page stories about dinosaurs and earthquakes and seeing-eye dogs, with questions at the end. The folders were called Power Builders and they were levelled according to colour—red, blue, yellow, orange, brown—all the way up to the dreamed-for, cheated-for purple. Power Builders came with their own answer keys, the idea being that you moved at your own rate and—we heard it a hundred times—that when you cheated, you only cheated yourself ... there were a dozen ... abbreviations, TTUM, FSU, PQB—all having to do with formulas that had reduced reading to a science.... By seventh grade, there was a special Development Reading class. (Mental reading, we called it.) The classroom was filled with audio-visual aids, phonetics charts, reading laboratories. Once a week, the teacher plugged in the speed-reading machine that projected a story on the board, one phrase at a time, faster and faster. Get a piece of dust in your eye—blink—and you were lost.

There were no books in the Developmental Reading room— the lab. Even in English class we escaped books easily.... All through high school, in fact, I read little except for magazines. Though I've started reading seriously now, in college, I still find myself drawn in bookstores to the bright covers and shiny, power-builder look. My eyes have been trained to skip nonessentials (adjectives, adverbs) and dart straight to the meaty phrases (TVPQM). But—perhaps in defiance of that whirring black rate-builder projector—it takes me three hours to read 100 pages.

Testing programmes in schools have tended to reinforce thinking about reading as a bundle of skills. In discussing measurement in reading Farr and Tuinman (1972) point out that researchers may state that reading is 'that collection of behaviours operationally defined by the test'. They suggest that in research on reading, operational definitions which relate the measure used to observables and/or abstractions out-side the measure itself are essential. A circular and limiting effect has occurred where the school has viewed tests as setting out the behaviours that compose reading. The use of results of some reading tests has concealed factors in the child's language that need attention. Often the tests have revealed deficits in the child's reading performance that cannot be overcome without adequate consideration of his language develop-ment. Schools have neglected to look further than the results of reading tests in developing programmes for reading improvement.

Wilkinson (1971) has made this statement:

> Learning to read is also, and centrally, a matter of language. Unless he has some language already, the child cannot read language. All the other variables in the situation, important though they may be, must be subordinate to this fact. Certainly 'reading readiness tests', for example, contain linguistic items—vocabulary, word matching, remembering the sequence of words in a story. But such tests tend to concentrate on vocabulary rather than syntax; they do not look at the child's knowledge of language, his awareness of the possibi-lities of language.... It would seem that a systematic study of reading and prereading oracy is one of the most important of our tasks over the next few years.

While schools use reading tests considerably in measuring the pupil's progress in reading, teachers recognize that these tests do not explain sufficiently the child's responses to reading. The teacher needs to reflect continuously on evidence of the child's language development to account for his reading growth. How well can he recall and restate an idea he has read? How well can he summarize a number of ideas from one source or from a number of sources? How well can he compare ideas within an article or between the article and his knowledge of reality? Often the child's failure to respond to reading suggests inadequate language ability prerequisite to the task. Has the child had sufficient experience synthesizing ideas in oral discussion to bring such a strategy to bear on the reading task? Has he had sufficient experience with concrete experiences where comparison was demanded to read critically? Can he bring the mind set and the language of comparison to reading tasks? The school's answer to the child's poor performance has often been to teach skills for which the child had insufficient oral language development.

> Again we become aware of the work children have to do (through language) before they can draw on the mature writer. If their talk and writing in the role of spectator does not reach occasionally beyond the level of gossip, how can they be expected to reach up

beyond that level into what the play, or the novel is saying. Yet it is at the level of gossip that we all start, and with many children the classroom offers them their only chance to move towards a fuller sense of what talk and reflection can offer. (Dixon 1967)

Testing programmes have often determined instructional procedures in reading. It is impossible to describe numerically the child's appreciation of what he reads, the intensity of his interest in reading, the success he experiences in using reading as a way of extending his real and imagined worlds, or his growing taste in literature. What can be reduced to statistical description has often been given precedence over these more elusive aspects of growth in reading.

The problem of changing school programmes so that they will accomplish language development for and through reading is not easily solved. Teachers often lack confidence in their intuitions about developing programmes. They have not been told clearly enough that:

If there is one generalization that can be made from research on developmental linguistics to date, it is that young human beings will have little trouble learning and producing language that is instrumental for goals that they see as important. (Entwisle 1971)

Preservice and in-service development of teachers needs to emphasize this generalization so that the teacher can recognize and resist forces that drive them in the direction of isolating the reading act from the rest of the child's growth and lead them to use procedures which have little relevance to the child.

Smith (1971) in *Understanding Reading* says:

The current instructional methods are probably not much inferior to the methods we shall develop as we learn more about learning to read. So many instructional methods have been tried, and so many succeed (in some instances at least), that further permutations in the game of instructional roulette are unlikely to produce any great gain, either by chance or design. What will make a difference is an understanding of the reading process.

Ways of working with teachers to develop this understanding of the reading process need exploration. The work of teacher developers would seem to be to nurture in the teacher a continuing desire to inquire into the process of language acquisition and reading. While the teacher needs to be informed about models of reading and language set out by researchers, she also needs to be able to observe and record development as it occurs in the children with whom she works. She needs to be trained in observing and documenting the child's changing language behaviour. At the same time she needs to examine the situations she develops in school to determine which of these are productive in helping the child grow as a user of language.

Schools and teachers will accept new descriptions of reading as a system of communications, will discard practices that isolate reading as a subject, will develop programmes to provide for the child's growth in reading as part of his language development, if they can be reassured and guided by authorities in the fields of reading research and curriculum change. Efforts to provide better instruction in reading call for increasing and closer contact of researchers and developers who generate new knowledge about reading and language with teachers who have intimate knowledge of children, their needs, and their potential.

*References*

ATHEY, IRENE (1971) Synthesis of papers on language development and reading *Reading Research Quarterly* 7, 1, 11

DIXON, JOHN (1967) *Growth Through English* London: Oxford University Press

ENTWISLE, D. R. (1971) Implications of language socialization for reading models and for learning to read *Reading Research Quarterly* 7, 1, 151

FARR, R. and TUINMAN, J. J. (1972) The dependent variable: measurement issues in reading research *Reading Research Quarterly* 7, 3, 413–423

MAYNARD, JOYCE (1972) *The New York Times Magazine* April 23rd

SMITH, F. (1971) *Understanding Reading: A Psycholinguistic Analysis of Reading and Learning to Read* New York: Holt, Rinehart and Winston

WILKINSON, ANDREW (1971) *The Foundations of Language, Talking and Reading in Young Children* London: Oxford University Press

# Part five Training the teachers of reading

## 14 You can't teach what you don't know

*Joyce M. Morris*

How can we ensure that all children in the United Kingdom are given the best possible opportunities to realize their potential for oracy and literacy? Suggested solutions to this perennial problem are manifold and rightly, in my view, include such reforms as universal nursery schooling plus a drastic reduction in the size of infant classes.

Clearly, most of the proposed changes in educational provision are too costly to carry out fully in the near future because of the economic situation. We must, of course, continue to press for reforms, especially those affecting the early years of childhood. But, at the same time, it is essential to convince the powers that be that what is most urgently needed is a marked increase in the total force of skilled, knowledgeable teachers of language and English in particular. That is, teachers in every sector of the educational system whose personal education and professional training have recognized at least two basic facts. First, language in spoken and written form is central to the educational process, and the skills involved have to be continuously fostered by expert teaching. Second, unlike other 'well-educated' citizens, it is not enough for teachers to have an operational knowledge of language arts and their uses: their knowledge must be explicit and cover, for example, salient characteristics of the English language, its phonology, orthography and so on.

At present, the nature and amount of explicit knowledge required to be an effective teacher of reading and related skills is not generally recognized. In fact, some influential people speak and write as though it is nonsensical to believe that any such knowledge is necessary. For instance Warnock (1972) made the following statement in a recent radio broadcast outlining her personal view of the James Report (DES 1972a):

Difficulties about status become more and more acute the further down the age-range the schools go, and nothing can ever eliminate the difference between a primary school teacher and, let us say, the teacher of mainly sixth-form pupils in a highly academic subject.

And not only is such a difference inevitable, it's also right. The academic teacher has something which the ordinary parent hasn't: namely, an academic knowledge of history, biology or whatever the subject may be.

As this kind of belief passes for informed opinion it is highly dangerous. We certainly can and must eliminate differences in the public status of teachers which arise from faulty notions about the nature of their respective tasks. It is simply not true that the younger or more backward the pupils the less the academic knowledge and intellectual discipline demanded of their teachers. It is also a disservice to the cause of education to give the tools of learning an inferior status to curriculum 'subjects' which apply these tools in the content fields.

Unfortunately, in the past teacher training establishments seem to have been brain-washed into accepting what is, fundamentally, intellectual snobbery. In consequence we have a situation where, for example, it would be unthinkable and, indeed, considered downright dangerous if the chemistry teachers in a secondary school and the authors of the textbooks being used had not proved themselves to have explicit knowledge of chemistry. Whereas it would not be unusual to find that the remedial reading teachers in the same school had no explicit knowledge of the reading process and had never even heard of phoneme-grapheme correspondence etc. Moreover, an examination of the published reading materials in use would almost certainly provide evidence that the knowledge of their authors was similarly inadequate. Thus, a school visitor from an underdeveloped country might justifiably conclude that, in our traditionally literate society, the effects of continued reading failure are less damaging to individuals than failure to learn sufficient chemistry to conduct a successful laboratory experiment.

By now you will have guessed that I have a bee in my bonnet about knowledge. Moreover, if you heard or have read my plenary paper at last year's conference (Morris 1972), you will realize that it is the same bee that stung me into advocating a revolution to overthrow a trio of tyrants called Ignorance, Confusion and Fear.

In the intervening period, these tyrants have suffered a little battering with the publication of a report (DES 1972b) which officially casts doubt on the existence of 'specific developmental dyslexia' as an identifiable syndrome. But, they recovered somewhat when the National Foundation for Educational Research (Start and Wells 1972), subsequently published results of the latest national reading survey and concluded:

At the end we are faced with the fact that reading standards today are no better than they were a decade ago and we have no hard experimental evidence from which we can explain why the postwar improvement has apparently ceased.

Hopefully, the Committee of Enquiry set up as one consequence of this report will make recommendations in 1974 which deal a fatal blow to Ignorance, Confusion and Fear. Meanwhile, let us look more closely at the proposition, 'you can't teach what you don't know'.

### 1 The abilities of 'successful' teachers

On commonsense grounds the proposition s valid, though to be precise the word 'successfully' needs to be inserted after the word 'teach'. Not surprisingly, practical experience and research findings support it. Maybe, however, we can best clarify the kinds of knowledge required by first considering the outstanding abilities of effective teachers of reading as revealed, for example, by the research I conducted at the NFER (Morris 1966) including some of it recently reported by colleagues (Cane and Smithers 1971).

### Establishing good relationships

Undoubtedly, to be successful, teachers must initially be able to establish good relationships with their pupils based on mutual respect and regard. For, in the absence of such conditions, little or no learning takes place and classroom chaos can reign supreme.

Here, the personality and experience of the teacher are of paramount importance. Even so, a necessary ingredient for success is skill in the practical application, to individuals and groups, of knowledge culled from the fields of educational psychology, child development and the social sciences generally.

### An analytical approach to the selection of methods, materials and media

Next we come to the first of the main abilities which depends on the kind of 'explicit' knowledge which, hitherto, has been comparatively neglected in the education and training of teachers. This is the ability to adopt an *analytical* approach to the selection of methods, materials and media.

Admittedly, in recent years, greater efforts have been made to inform teachers about the range and type of methods, materials and media available. But such information is not very useful unless accompanied by the acquisition of knowledge which enables them to choose wisely not only to suit children's needs in particular circumstances but to reject what is unsound from a linguistic point of view. Furthermore, as you will see later from the order in which I summarize some of the kinds of knowledge required, I believe that in teacher training it is essential to correct the tendency to put 'the cart before the horse'. That is, students should be trained to understand the substance of English language teaching as a prelude to getting to grips with the 'how', 'with what', and 'through which' of methods, materials and media respectively.

### Structuring appropriate learning situations

To be effective, teachers must also structure appropriate learning situations, and this requires organizational ability based on a knowledge of what has to be learnt at different stages in the acquisition of language skills.

Knowledgeable teachers do not imagine that the cause of oracy is being adequately served by encouraging children to express themselves freely in classroom chatter. They are consciously aware of the various uses of spoken language and provide specific opportunities for guided practice in all of them. Open-plan schools notwithstanding, they arrange quiet periods in which to develop auditory discrimination, aural comprehension and critical listening skills.

With regard to literacy, there is no nonsense about reading being a 'natural' process with the concomitant, erroneous idea that a teacher's responsibility virtually stops with the provision of a 'rich' reading environment and time to hear children read every day. Knowledge also prevents misunderstandings about the relationships between speech and print, and helps teachers to appreciate the confusion caused by dialect differences especially those which differ markedly from 'standard' English speech and writing. Hence, knowledgeable teachers realize that a language-experience approach is just an 'approach', and will not take children far on the road to literacy unless they structure learning situations which lead to the goal of being able to read and write standard English or close approximations to it.

### Giving systematic diagnostic instruction

Additionally, effective teachers assess and record the progress of individual pupils, diagnose their difficulties, and give systematic instruction when and where it is needed. However, none of these practices is possible without explicit knowledge of the type intimated so far, and some of which I now proceed to spell out albeit in summary form.

### 2  Some of the 'explicit' knowledge required

In my opinion, the preservice course for all teachers should begin with a never to be forgotten series of lecture-debates on the role of language in human affairs generally and education in particular.

### Principal uses of language

Such a series might well start with discussion of the principal uses of language because this naturally leads to the clarification of teaching objectives. Though the uses may be listed separately as follows, usually more than one use is involved in a given utterance:

1 The most obvious use of language is *to communicate* information, thoughts and ideas with a maximum of accuracy and a minimum of effort.

2 Language is used *to express* emotions as a release from tensions or a reaction to emergencies. Examples include 'swear' words and some lyric poetry. Much of the activity known as children's creative writing also serves a 'cathartic' or 'therapeutic' purpose since deciphering is necessary before communication is possible

3 Language is used *to socialize* i.e. to keep the social wheels oiled and moving. For instance we say 'Good morning' when it may be raining hard, and 'How do you do?' when not expecting an answer.

4 Language is used *to think* with. Here, student teachers should understand that thinking is controlled by the qualities and categories of one's native language.

5 Language is used *to control* the behaviour of others. This is an inescapable fact of life especially the professional life of teachers, politicians, advertisers and so on. Moreover, a good deal of the stress of a teacher's probationary year could be prevented by expert training in this use of language.

## Salient characteristics of spoken English

From language uses, student teachers could logically move on to the salient characteristics of spoken English. Briefly, their studies should cover:

1 The historical origins of modern English as a background for making word study fascinating even for infants.

2 Dialects (regional and social), idiolects and registers to prepare, at least, for the likelihood of children's confusion stemming from these differences.

3 A scientific description of the levels of English e.g. its phonology, lexis and grammar as a basis, primarily, for understanding the linguistic achievements of entrants to reception classes.

4 Implications of the four grammars of English namely, schoolbook, classical, structural and transformational. For example, schoolbook grammar, based on the Latin model, ignores speech, whereas structural grammar begins with the basic unit of sound contrast i.e. the phoneme. Moreover, structuralists have developed a special technique of analysis called the 'slot and substitution' method which British teachers will encounter in studies of reading primers such as that recently reported by Reid (1970).

## Children's acquisition of speech

Next I suggest that prospective teachers study the stages of speech

H

development of the normally-hearing child as summarized by Whetnall and Fry (1971). Though space will not allow reproduction of the summary, I quote stages five to nine inclusive to illustrate how such knowledge could help to dispel prevalent misconceptions about the 'analytic' and 'rule-learning' language abilities of reception class children:

5 He has learned to recognize sounds coming in as belonging to one of forty phonemic categories and he has learned to make sounds appropriate to the categories when he is sending speech out.

6 He has learned how to string phonemes together to make morphemes and words.

7 He has acquired a vocabulary of morphemes and words which form the basis of his speech and has a passive vocabulary far in excess of this.

8 He has learned the rules according to which morphemes and words are put together to form sentences.

9 He has collected considerable knowledge of the statistics of word and sentence formation which he applies in the reception of speech.

From speech to print

Since all this has been achieved by nearly every normal child by the age of five or six, infant teachers have much on which to build a foundation for literacy. However, before they can do this in a professional manner they, and indeed all literacy teachers, must have detailed knowledge of the relationships and differences between speech and print at various levels of the language.

Hence, I suggest that the next part of the preservice course should be devoted to topics such as phoneme-grapheme correspondence which, at present, teachers are not usually obliged to consider unless they plan to adopt a regularized writing system such as ita. It should also end with a full realization of why learning to read and write is generally a markedly harder task for children than learning to understand and use spoken language.

Language processes and pedagogy

By now students should have sufficient knowledge about language to digest details of what might be called 'language processes and pedagogy'. Here, the nature of listening, speaking, reading and writing must be fully understood before considering teaching techniques.

Limitations of space will only permit a reminder that having so far followed the kind of course outlined, students would recognize the need for analytic as well as nonanalytic techniques in the development of word recognition skills. What is more, they would accept that most infants are capable of profiting from expert instruction in phonic and structural analysis in addition to the customary encouragement to use picture, configuration and context clues.

## Children's literature
Of course, throughout their training, prospective teachers should be encouraged to get to know a great deal about children's publications far beyond the realm and necessary limitations of basal readers. Indeed children's literature, including much that goes into the 'reference' category, has to be recognized as an integral part of language teaching in so far as it represents both a strong motivating force to master skills and a rich reward for achievement.

## Prospect
At last, my 'knowledge bee' has stopped buzzing though it will surely sting me into action again when I meet those tyrants, Ignorance, Confusion and Fear. Certainly, it will make its presence felt during discussions of the James Report, *Teacher Education and Training* (DES 1972a).

On the whole, I agree with the report's recommendations concerning in-service provision, but feel that those for preservice provision, if implemented, could eventually leave us in a worse situation than today with regard to teachers of reading and related skills. Unless the proposed two years of higher education before professional training had a strong, compulsory language component, such as I have indicated above, I fear there will be a higher proportion of teachers who are unsuccessful because they try to teach what they don't know.

## References
CANE, B. and SMITHERS, J. (1971) *The Roots of Reading* Slough: National Foundation for Educational Research

DES (1972a) *Teacher Education and Training* (James Report) London: HMSO

DES (1972b) *Children with Specific Reading Difficulties* (Tizard Report) London: HMSO

MORRIS, J. M. (1966) *Standards and Progress in Reading* Slough: NFER

MORRIS, J. M. (1972) 'From speech to print and back again' in V. Southgate (ed) *Literacy at all Levels* London: Ward Lock Educational

REID, J. F. (1970) Sentence structure in reading primers *Research in Education No. 3* Manchester: Manchester University Press

START, K. B. and WELLS, B. K. (1972) *The Trend of Reading Standards* Slough: National Foundation for Educational Research

WARNOCK, M. (1972) Mary Warnock asks: is school teaching a mystery? *The Listener* April 20th

WHETNALL, E. and FRY, D. B. (1971) *The Deaf Child* London: Heinemann

## 15 Training the teachers of reading in England and Wales

*Vera Southgate*

### Introduction

However diverse the views held by educators about children learning to read, most would agree on the importance of the role played by the teacher and his or her training, experience and expertise. Thus teacher training, both initial and in-service, is a crucial issue and probably the single most important factor affecting the reading ability and general language development of children, students and the whole adult population.

In December 1970, a Committee of Enquiry into Teacher Education and Training in England and Wales was set up by the Secretary of State for Education and Science, under the chairmanship of Lord James of Rusholme. Its brief was to enquire into the present arrangements for the education, training and probation of teachers in England and Wales, to examine three particular questions related to this subject and to make recommendations. Only the first question is of direct relevance here as it concerned the content and organization of the courses to be provided. It was in this context that in March 1971 the writer presented written evidence to the committee (Southgate 1971). This evidence, which has not previously been published, forms the main content of this paper.

### Written evidence to the James Committee

The following is a summary of the paper, entitled *Reading and the Language Arts* (Memorandum and recommendations on the content of courses provided in colleges of education), presented to the James Committee.

### The scope of the subject

Learning to read is a developmental process which extends from infancy to adulthood and is closely related to the other language arts, listening, speaking, and writing. Moreover, reading is not a unitary skill but a combination of many subskills, some of which can only be mastered within the field of higher education. The component skills contributing to the skill of reading have been analysed in a variety of ways by different reading experts. They generally include developmental skills, consisting of a range of skills in the mechanics of reading and in reading comprehension, accompanied by additional skills relating to functional reading and recreational reading. The skills of writing, speaking and listening could also be divided into many subskills. The inculcation of literacy and oracy across such a broad spectrum is clearly a matter which should concern teachers of all ages of pupils and of most subjects, as well as a large proportion of the staffs in teacher training establishments.

## Reading in the United Kingdom

In the United Kingdom the subject of reading and the language arts has in the past been narrowly defined and usually confined to beginning reading skills. Being regarded as an activity relating to infants and backward older pupils, it is assumed to be the responsibility of only infant teachers, remedial teachers and those college lecturers concerned with methods of teaching younger or backward children. Furthermore, reading is rarely considered to be a subject worthy of serious study at university level, in contrast to America, Canada and certain European countries where there are university departments devoted to the advanced study of reading and the language arts. The result is that in Britain the subject of reading lacks status.

On the other hand many teachers, particularly at the primary level, are conscious of the importance of children learning to read and are usually eager to increase their own expertise. Teachers' in-service courses on reading are generally well attended and frequently oversubscribed. Although many such courses are provided, teachers continually ask for more. The national survey of in-service training undertaken by the Department of Education and Science (1970) showed how the demand for courses on reading far exceeded the provision made, whilst Bolam (1971) also reported similar requests from probationer teachers. Such requests from both newly-appointed and experienced teachers must be regarded as an indication of certain inadequacies in the initial training of teachers in this respect.

Even so, teachers' pleas for reading courses and their suggestions that students should receive more reading training, refer mainly to the early stages of reading. Teachers at the upper primary and secondary levels seldom regard it as their specific function to extend the initial skills of literacy to more advanced levels, nor have they usually been trained to do so.

If it is considered important that children, students and other adults should attain the highest possible levels of mastery of language skills, our conception of this area of the curriculum will need extending in respect of the content, and the range of both those who study it and those who teach it.

Existing practices in colleges of education

In many colleges, work in reading and the language arts is limited in the following respects:

1. the number of students who study it
2. its coverage of the total subject matter
3. the time devoted to it
4. the range of lecturers contributing to its study
5. the expertise of the lecturers concerned.

A brief examination of these five limiting factors will serve to highlight existing practices in the majority of teacher training establishments in England and Wales.

Lecturers on reading and the other skills of literacy, as well as practical experience in teaching them, are mainly confined to students taking infant or infant/junior courses. The majority of students who anticipate teaching older children neither study the language skills in detail nor have practical experience in teaching them. Yet as we are well aware, many teachers do not eventually teach children of the ages on whom their training was centred. Furthermore, in whatever sort of educational establishment the student eventually teaches, he will find pupils who require tuition, at some level, in the skills of literacy.

For the student who does study reading in college, the syllabus is likely to be concentrated on beginning reading and remedial reading. The inclusion of the development of intermediate and higher order skills in reading or the extension of the curriculum to include a detailed study of the other language arts is exceptional.

The general narrowness of the language arts curriculum reflects the limited amount of time usually devoted to this subject. For example, in 1967 in colleges within one area training organization, students following infant or infant/junior courses received only an average of twelve hours' tuition in beginning reading during their whole time in college. The range extended from three to six hours up to thirty to thirty-five hours. Students taking junior/secondary and secondary courses received considerably less reading instruction or none at all. In addition, in about half the colleges a few hours were devoted to remedial reading.

The limited number of college lecturers engaged in literacy training is a direct outcome of the prevalent narrow conception of the subject matter. In many colleges lecturers in English do not participate in this work which is left to education lecturers and sometimes solely to those concerned with infant method.

It is probable that many lecturers actually engaged in reading training would not claim to be experts even in beginning reading, much less in the later development and uses of reading skills. It is encouraging, however, to note that lecturers in English as well as in education are becoming more aware of the need to increase their own expertise in the language arts, in order to broaden the programmes of their students. For example, a twenty-five session course entitled 'Teaching for literacy', arranged in 1967–8 for college lecturers within the Manchester area training organization, was attended by twenty-nine education lecturers and fifteen English lecturers.

## Recommendations

First, all student teachers should be expected to undertake a broadly based introductory course concerned with reading and the language arts at all educational levels. It should include, and might even begin with, an examination of the skills which contribute to efficient adult reading and an assessment of the student's own levels of competence in these areas. Attention should be drawn to average standards at different ages, the range of attainments to be expected within each age group, and to simple initial assessments of the reading attainments of whole classes.

Second, all students should also take at least two further courses on selected aspects of the subject at different age levels. The following are examples of such courses which might be available:

1 beginning reading
2 the failing reader
3 extending the study skills in the middle school
4 training children to use dictionaries, reference books and encyclopedias—at different levels
5 using the library effectively—at different stages
6 the appreciation and evaluation of what is read
7 different methods of recording information gathered from reference books—at middle or secondary school levels
8 encouraging creative writing at different levels.

Third, in addition, all students should undertake some practical work in the language arts with children of different ages. This practical work could be closely related to the student's selected courses from the optional list.

Fourth, as a student is unlikely either to gain the maximum benefit from his college studies or to become an efficient teacher unless he himself is proficient in the language arts, arrangements should be made for student tuition in those skills in which he is weak. This recommendation is tantamount to suggesting that every teacher training establishment requires a small remedial department for students—an accepted practice in colleges and universities in the USA. (It should be noted that the mere recognition that not all adults are equally proficient in all the language skills would emphasize the scope of the subject, reinforce the idea of its relevance for all students and teachers and increase students' interest in helping children to gain maximum proficiency.)

Fifth, a broad curriculum in reading and the language arts could only be offered if lecturers in English and education would combine with tutor-librarians and if many more lecturers were prepared to increase their own knowledge. Thus more advanced courses in the language arts, both part-time and full-time, would need to be provided by the Department of Education and Science and by universities.

Sixth, one final recommendation concerns the support university schools of education should give to college lecturers in this work. Departments of language arts should be established in a number of universities, geographically dispersed. They should be staffed not only with experts in all the language arts, linguisticians and educational psychologists, but also with people having experience of schools and teacher training establishments. Such departments could offer one year university diploma courses in reading and the language arts, to college lecturers in the first instance, and later to experienced teachers intend-ing to become lecturers or advisers. In addition, the subjects offered could form part of the syllabus for higher degrees. These departments would also be concerned with undertaking research and with the dis-semination of knowledge to lecturers, advisers, teachers and students.

*The James Report*

The recommendations of the James Report (DES 1972), which was published in January 1972, related mainly to the second and third aspects of its brief and thus few references were made to the actual subjects of college courses. Even so, the importance of the language arts was mentioned in connection with both initial and in-service training, as shown in the following quotations:

> In such a hubbub of competing priorities it may not be surprising, although it is certainly alarming, that such matters as the teaching of reading should sometimes appear to be neglected. The assertion that such essentially relevant and practical elements are not presented with sufficient clarity and emphasis is widespread. It may be con-cluded that, with things as they are, the colleges are asked to do too much, are left with no rational basis for discrimination and are often unable to give enough time to aspects of training which they and the profession recognize as central.
>
> Teachers in the primary school—and those in secondary schools who are faced with illiteracy or semiliteracy in their pupils—will need to continue to improve their understanding and competence in the language arts, i.e. language development and the teaching of reading and writing. Although this deeper understanding, however much emphasized in initial training, cannot be fully acquired with-

out prolonged experience, suitable in-service training, rooted in the experience teachers have already had, can be a powerful aid.

(Note how this second quotation limits itself to beginning reading and remedial reading.)

Elsewhere in the report it is suggested that regional and/or national language centres might be set up and that certain university departments might specialize in certain subjects in which they would become centres of excellence—which is in line with one of the proposals in the writer's evidence to this committee.

*Recent developments in teacher training*

In the eighteen months since the writer's evidence was prepared for the James Committee, the growing interest of college lecturers in the language arts, mentioned in this evidence, has continued to increase. Two recent conferences and the provision of two additional advanced courses confirm this trend. At the UKRA Annual Conference in Manchester in July 1971, lecturers formed the largest category of delegates and a special study group for lecturers numbered eighty. A report on this study group, written by the convenor Margaret Clark (1972) appears in the published conference proceedings.

The second residential conference entitled 'Training the Teachers of Reading', arranged by the School of Education of Manchester University in conjunction with UKRA, was held in April 1972. It was attended by 120 lecturers from seventy-six different teacher training establishments from all over the United Kingdom. Discussions at this conference confirmed that lecturers are eager to increase their own expertise, that more reading courses are being planned for all students, that these courses aim to cover a greater proportion of the total field of the language arts and that additional time is being allocated to them.

At this particular conference, attention was concentrated on the content of courses and ways in which students could gain practical experience in teaching the language arts. Ideas from different colleges on experimental schemes for providing such practical experience were pooled. They included the following.

Children were often brought into colleges. Sometimes whole classes came and students observed both teachers and lecturers teaching the children, and often participated in the teaching themselves. In another case backward readers from a junior school in an educational priority area came to college one afternoon per week and each was tutored by an individual student.

In other instances students worked with children in schools for one half-day a week for one or two terms. Students were generally given responsibility for individual children or for small groups, and their work involved studying children's reading attainments and difficulties and devising interesting ways of encouraging and helping them to read. Some students prepared simple individual readers for junior children who had failed to learn to read, while others combined handmade books with creative activities. In one college, students had recorded stories and used these with slow readers in conjunction with simple handmade readers based on the stories. A certain amount of work by students had been linked with radio and television reading programmes.

Such continuous long-term contacts between children and students were proving beneficial to both. These contacts also reinforced the practical work undertaken on teaching practice, which itself showed signs of focusing more attention on language arts. During school practice periods special assignments were often set for students. Two examples of such assignments were keeping detailed reading records of a number of children, gathering information about their home backgrounds, relating this to reading and planning work to help the children; and considering the development of reading skills within the context of topic work.

In some areas pressure from colleges on nearby schools made it difficult to provide students with sufficient face to face contacts with children. The following suggestion was made for partially overcoming this problem, while still focusing students' attention on practical aspects of organization. Data could be collected from an actual class of children and a range of simulation exercises based on it; for example, possible grouping of children, suggestions of teaching strategies required, matching reading materials to children's attainments, record keeping, allocation of teacher time, and considering child directed activities.

Other ideas and experiences exchanged on this course related to workshop sessions for students and to the uses of tape recorders, video tapes, teaching machines and multimedia packages.

The academic year 1972–73 will see the beginning of two additional advanced reading courses. In September 1972 a one year full-time course, leading to a diploma in the teaching of reading of the University of Sheffield, will begin at Totley-Thornbridge college of education, under the direction of William Latham. In January 1973 the Open University will be offering a course in reading development under the direction of Professor John Merritt. Both courses are planned for experienced teachers and lecturers and will undoubtedly contribute to the supply of knowledgeable people available for staffing future courses of teacher training in the language arts.

## The Bullock Committee

Meanwhile, following on the heels of the publication of the NFER's report *The Trend of Reading Standards* (Start and Wells 1972) which suggested a decline, or at least a levelling out, of reading standards in eleven and fifteen year old pupils, and in the light of growing public interest in questions of reading and language development, the Secretary of State for Education and Science has recently set up a Committee of Enquiry into Reading and the Use of English, under the chairmanship of Sir Alan Bullock, Vice-Chancellor of Oxford University. Its terms of reference are as follows:

To consider in relation to schools:
a  all aspects of teaching the use of English including reading, writing and speech;
b  how present practice might be improved, and the role that initial and in-service training might play;
c  to what extent arrangements for monitoring the general level of attainment in these skills can be introduced or improved;
and to make recommendations.

The committee held its first meeting in June 1972 and hopes to publish its report in the spring of 1974. As this is the first government inquiry into the teaching of reading and English in England and Wales for fifty years and as teacher training is specifically referred to in the brief, its recommendations will clearly be of great importance to all lecturers in teacher training establishments and will, no doubt, be anticipated with interest.

*Conclusion*
The writer feels certain that the newly-awakened interest in reading and other aspects of language development, which in the past few years has begun to reassert itself in England and Wales, (in Scotland it never fell from grace) will continue to increase. It seems reasonable to predict that in schools, teacher training establishments and the field of in-service training the next decade will see a rapidly growing emphasis on this aspect of the curriculum to which so many of us already accord very high priority.

*References*
BOLAM, R. (1971) Guidance for probationer teachers in *Trends in Education* 21, 41–48
CLARK, M. M. (1972) 'Training the teachers of reading' in V. Southgate (ed) *Literacy at all Levels* London: Ward Lock Educational
DES (1970) *Survey of In-Service Training for Teachers* (Special Statistical Report No 552) London: HMSO
DES (1972) *Teacher Education and Training* (James Report) London: HMSO
SOUTHGATE, V. (1971) *Reading and the Language Arts* Unpublished paper (Memorandum and recommendations on the content of courses pro-

vided in colleges of education), submitted as written evidence to the James Committee

START, K. B. and WELLS, B. K. (1972) *The Trend of Reading Standards* Slough: National Foundation for Educational Research

# 16  The college of education reading centre and the practising teacher

*William Latham*

## Introduction

Sir Ronald Gould is quoted as having said that 'no teacher can afford to spend a working lifetime relying on the capital he has acquired in the years of initial training' (Schools Council 1970). The implication of this statement would appear to be that there is a need for teachers to have the opportunity to learn about, experiment with, and evaluate ideas that may be new to them, concerning curricula and methods.

In this paper a way of partially meeting the above needs through a reading centre in a college of education will be described and discussed.

## Teachers centres

The concept of a teachers centre, a place where teachers could go in order to increase their professional knowledge is not new. Indeed, it has been suggested that 'a little research would almost certainly reveal activities as far back as the early 1920s that had some of the characteristics of teachers centres today' (Schools Council 1970). Such centres were, however, uncommon until a sudden increase in provision after 1965 had raised the number to over three hundred by 1968. The increase in number between 1965 and 1968 was associated with the work of the Schools Council.

The Schools Council was set up in 1964, its terms of reference being 'to carry out research and development work on curricula, teaching methods and examinations in primary and secondary schools' (Schools Council 1967).

It was soon realized that if the work of the Council was to have impact in terms of changes in educational practice, then answers would have to be found to the following questions:

1 How could maximum involvement of teachers in the work of research and development be obtained?
2 How could the knowledge obtained from the Council's projects be passed to teachers?

In an attempt to find an answer to these questions, the Council, in a working paper (Schools Council 1965), advocated the setting-up of local centres to make the Schools Council's working papers, projects, and other activities the focal point for local discussion and curriculum development. It was after the publication of this paper that the rapid increase in the number of teachers centres began.

Whilst, undoubtedly, the work of the Council led to the rapid increase in the number of teachers centres, it did not necessarily dominate the thinking of those responsible for the centres. As is typical of educational institutions in this country, the centres came to differ widely in activities. It can, however, be said that despite diversity in practice, the role of the centres was seen, in theory at least, as involving *all* curricula and *all* methods.

### The role of the reading centre

The reading centre differs from the teachers centre in that it is, as its name implies, a specialist centre concerned with the teaching of reading.

The justification for a specialist centre concerned with the teaching of reading, as opposed to seeing the matter as *one* of the concerns of a teachers centre, is two-fold. First, the importance of reading as a key to academic success and successful participation in adult society, and second, the evidence from surveys suggesting slow progress in the post-war period towards prewar standards of reading attainment (Georgiades and Latham 1967) and, more recently, of a regression from the level reached in the 1960s (Start and Wells 1972).

### A reading centre in a college of education

Totley-Thornbridge College of Education, in which the centre to be described is situated, is a college of approximately 1,000 students. It offers courses of training for teaching at levels ranging from nursery to secondary school. The college also offers a course leading to a diploma in the teaching of reading.

### The aim of the centre

The aim of the centre is to help teachers to produce efficient readers, who also have a positive attitude to reading for purposes of study and for pleasure. In as far as study is concerned, the efficient reader may be considered to be one who has skills related to:

1 The finding of sources of information relevant to purpose.
2 The abstraction of relevant information—this implies literal understanding and making inferences.
3 The retention of the material obtained in a form that makes it available for future use.
4 The adjustment of speed of reading to material and purpose.

In summary, 'the efficient reader possesses skills relevant to finding, understanding and using information. He is also able, by adjusting speed of reading to material and purpose, to reduce the time required to obtain knowledge to a personal minimum' (Latham 1970).

If one considers the characteristics of the efficient reader it is obvious that we are dealing with skills at adult level. But such adult skills must, necessarily, rest upon a foundation of lower order skills (e.g. word recognition, phonic analysis and synthesis), and the positive attitude to books which one also wishes to obtain must arise from early experiences of reading which are associated with pleasure and success. Thus, if the centre is to fulfil its aim, it is necessary that learning to read be conceptualized, by those associated with it, as a long-term process and, as with any process which continues throughout childhood into adult life, a developmental process.

Examination of learning to read as a long-term developmental process (Latham 1968) suggests that the following separate, but related ideas, are involved:

1 Learning to read is seen as one aspect of the sequence of related changes which follow one another as the child progresses from birth to maturity. Development in reading is seen as being closely related to physical, intellectual, social and emotional development.
2 Learning to read is seen, in common with other aspects of the child's development, to be sequential, having its roots in preschool life and language experience and proceeding through lower order decoding skills to the higher order study skills of the adult reader.
3 Learning to read is seen as closely related to learning to listen, speak, and write with writing forming a bridge between speaking and reading.

The result of accepting learning to read as a long-term developmental process is, as far as the centre is concerned, two-fold. First, it means that the centre must be equipped with materials concerned with learning to listen and to speak as well as to read—and also with materials concerned with writing as a bridge between speaking and reading. Second, the services of the centre must be available to teachers and teachers to be, associated with all stages within the educational system.

*Opening the centre to teachers*
One aspect of the work of the centre is concerned with its role as a resources centre for students. Another aspect is the services it offers to teachers within the schools to which it sends students. This paper is mainly concerned with this second aspect of the centre's work.

The first move which led to the opening of the centre to teachers was sending a letter to the teachers concerned. The letter contained tentative suggestions about services that the centre might offer, and asked the teachers to comment on these and to make further suggestions. The letter also asked for convenient dates on which a meeting might be held to discuss the whole matter.

As a result of the meeting, guidelines for the work of the centre were drawn up.

*The role of the centre as an aid to teachers*
The present role of the centre is outlined below:

1  It acts as a resources centre, exhibiting as wide a range of materials as possible.
2  It offers information concerning the use of materials and their possible value, on the basis of information from controlled research and/or school use.

To implement this latter aspect of the role of the centre the following procedures are followed:

1  The centre is open to teachers at set times, or by appointment. A member of the college staff is available for consultation concerning the use of materials, and what is known concerning their possible value.
2  Pamphlets are produced for sale to teachers.
3  Teachers are invited to attend talks by visiting speakers on different aspects of the language skills.
4  Teachers are encouraged, and helped, to evaluate their own methods, and materials new to them, within the setting of their school.
5  Display space is offered to teachers wishing to exhibit new ideas they have developed.

The outline of the role of the centre does not include prescribing for teachers the 'best' methods or materials. The omission of this possible aspect of the work of the centre may seem controversial. In my view to make decisions of this kind for teachers is derogatory to their professional role. To collect information and to help with its evaluation is an acceptable role for the centre; to take the evaluation and final decision-making out of the hands of the qualified teacher is not.

Display and storage
In converting a bare space into a viable reading centre the following points were borne in mind:

1  The need to maximize horizontal and vertical display space, with the intention of highlighting aspects of the teaching of reading by exhibitions which would have a life span of about five weeks.

I

2 The need to emphasize in storage ease of access to materials and ease of return to the place from which they were obtained.

Concerning (2) above, plastic containers were used which were arranged in alphabetical order of contents, in rows beneath the horizontal display surfaces. These containers could be removed when the contents were required and the resultant gap in the alphabetical order offered a guide to correct return. Where some of the materials related to a particular container were too large for the container (e.g. large flash cards associated with a reading series), these could be stored in a cupboard in the centre, and the appropriate container could contain a card indicating that further materials might be found in the cupboard.

Tea trolleys were used, beneath which materials could be stored, and their tops could be used to spread out materials for examination. These trolleys could also be used to transport materials round the college.

*Advantages of a college of education setting*
The following advantages may be claimed for a reading centre in a college of education setting:

1 The teaching of reading, seen as a long-term development process, requires an interdisciplinary approach by people with practical experience of teaching at different levels. Such an approach becomes easier when the people concerned are working together on the same campus.
2 It is desirable to exhibit, or have available, the largest possible selection of materials. The range can be considerably extended if the resources of the centre can be added to easily when required. This is possible in a college of education where, for example, the English and technology of education departments can have links with the reading centre.
3 The strengthening of the links between, and the creating of greater understanding amongst, teacher, student, and college of education lecturer is highly desirable. A college reading centre provides a focal point for the necessary interaction.

*Summary and conclusion*
A brief description has been given of the development of teachers centres, and the case for the establishment of specialist centres concerned with the teaching of reading has been put forward. The need to see learning to read as a long-term developmental process, and the effect of so doing on the stocking and functioning of such a centre has been considered.

The opening and functions of such a centre in a college of education in relation to serving teachers have been described, and the advantages of a college setting have been stressed.

This brief account of the reading centre at Craigie College of Education, Ayr, is based on the booklet prepared for the ninth annual study conference of the United Kingdom Reading Association.

*References*

GEORGIADES, N. J. and LATHAM, W. (1967) Letter in *Reading* 1, 2

LATHAM, W. (1968) Are today's teachers adequately trained in the teaching of reading? *Third International Reading Symposium* London: Cassell

LATHAM, W. (1970) Higher order reading skills *Teaching Reading: Ace Forum No. 4* London: Ginn

SCHOOLS COUNCIL (1965) *Raising the School Leaving Age: A Co-operative Programme of Research and Development* Working Paper No. 2 London: HMSO

SCHOOLS COUNCIL (1967) *Curriculum Development: Teachers' Groups and Centres* London: HMSO

SCHOOLS COUNCIL (1970) *Teachers Centres and the Changing Curriculum* London: HMSO

START, K. B. and WELLS, B. K. (1972) *The Trend of Reading Standards* Slough: National Foundation for Educational Research

*ERRATUM*
The final paragraph on page 127 should appear as the final paragraph on page 132.

# 17  A reading centre - impact and potential

*Alastair Hendry*

## Introduction

There are clearly wide differences among colleges of education in Britain in the number of departments involved in courses in the teaching of reading, the time allocated to such courses, the amount of continuing teaching experience of tutors, the training methods used and the resources available for this work. It is precisely in these areas that a college reading centre has considerable potential value. As new reading centres are being established both in Scotland and England, the time is perhaps opportune to provide an outline of the developments of a reading centre in Craigie College so that others may share our experience, avoid the flaws which they may see in our organization and respond with comments and suggestions. We hope it will provide an adequate impression of the impact such a unit can make.

## Initial stages

In June 1969, the Principal of Craigie College invited lecturers from the departments of infant and primary education together with a member of the college library staff to plan the setting up of a reading centre to be used by the different college departments in their work with both students and teachers on the teaching of reading at all levels of the primary school.

With the guidance of various heads of departments, the tutors responsible set about building up a comprehensive stock of materials and equipment. Appropriate furniture for display and working surfaces were designed and constructed with the help of a college technician. A system of room dividers was developed to enable complete flexibility in the use of the centre.

## Facilities

As the reading centre was set up to meet certain clearly recognized and frequently expressed needs, the tutors in their planning sought to arrange for the provision of a wide range of facilities which would both contribute to the preservice training of students and, at the same time, render assistance to teachers in service. After two years, the facilities remain the same, but the scope is vastly greater and the service more extensive, and we hope, more efficient.

Preservice

From the start, our aim was to provide for students:

1 opportunities to work with children
2 a supply of the most important published material for their consideration
3 opportunities for making materials relevant to their work with children
4 an opportunity to examine and use apparatus and equipment in the teaching of reading
5 material which may be used by students to develop their own reading skills
6 illustrative examples of work produced by children
7 a selection of articles, journals and books for private study.

In-service

The centre welcomes visits from individual teachers or groups and provides:

1 opportunities for the discussion of and instruction in different approaches and equipment
2 exchange of ideas, experience and techniques relevant to particular reading difficulties
3 a supply of published material for consideration
4 opportunities for making materials relevant to the classroom situation
5 a meeting place for welcoming visiting lecturers
6 a means of feedback on the efficacy of approaches encouraged
7 the possibilities for research programmes and 'action research'.

*Resources available*

As the approach to the teaching of reading in Craigie College is a developmental one, i.e. students in lectures, seminars and workshop situations, as well as on teaching practice, become familiar with the entire sequence from the prereading stage in infants to reading in the upper primary, a wide range of stock is provided. This includes:

1 materials for prereading activities, e.g. prereading books and film strips, reading schemes at present in use, together with those most recently published (with all supplementary books, pictures, cards, manuals)
2 current approaches to the teaching of reading, e.g. *Words in Colour, Breakthrough to Literacy,* ita
3 structured materials such as Stott's *Programmed Reading Kit,* SRA

*Reading Laboratories,* Pilot Libraries, *English Colour Code,* Ward Lock Educational *Reading Workshops*

4  attainment and diagnostic tests (such as might be used by the teacher)
5  books produced specifically for children with difficulties in reading (most series in print)
6  audio-visual equipment, tape recorders, Language Master, film strips, video-tape, games, apparatus, tape/slide sychronized units and Dictaloop
7  fiction and reference books appropriate for class libraries and topic work at different stages in the primary school (used in consideration of development of higher order skills).

As the volume of new books and related materials published each year continues to grow steadily, some selection of material for the centre becomes essential and the inclusion of this material depends upon various criteria, not least being its appropriateness and relevance to the classroom situation and available financial resources.

*Organization and use*

From the outset, Craigie Reading Centre has been simply a work area for the whole college, not the province of any one department. Its resources and equipment are independent of the college library stock and, not being borrowable, are permanently available for use. It has thus provided an ideal focus for the work done by, and for, the different departments on the teaching of reading.

As reading centre space is limited, students and staff tutors are asked to arrange their visits in advance with the centre secretary indicating both when they would like to visit and what books and materials they require. A library assistant has the special responsibility of setting out the materials for use at the times arranged.

Preservice

There have emerged three levels of such work. First, *departmental level.* Tutors from a department work with a group of students on specific reading topics. For example, infant education tutors and students examine in detail the content and rationale of the reading schemes in the schools used for teaching practice. (All diploma students are introduced to the teaching of the initial stages of reading and spend at least one teaching practice in an infant department.)

Primary education tutors and students consider techniques and materials (including audio-visual equipment) used in helping children who have difficulty in reading.

Second, *student level.* Students work in groups and individually on a variety of assignments. For example third year students for the English

Department consider in groups various types of children's fiction (picture books, historical fiction, fairy tales, 'best sellers').

Interdisciplinary studies explore a variety of topics, from *Breakthrough to Literacy* and *Words in Colour* to SRA *Reading Laboratories* and remedial techniques. Individual students from each year group examine relevant reading materials before and during teaching practices.

Guidance and practice in writing are provided for students about to work in schools where ita is the medium for early reading.

Final year students, before leaving college, familiarize themselves thoroughly with the materials and reading series in use in the schools to which they have been appointed.

A sample of first year students has been participating in a research project studying the effectiveness of the SRA *Reading Laboratory IVa* programme as an aid to the developing of reading skills at college level.

Third, *pupil level*. While the group of tutors mainly associated with the centre spend most of their time visiting students or working in schools themselves, the centre also provides facilities for work with school pupils. Nonreaders from a local school visited the centre regularly and were given assistance by students under the guidance of psychology department tutors.

The gradual emergence of this focus for all work in reading is of considerable significance for curricular development within a college. Immediate bonuses are communication amongst departments and coordination of effort. For Craigie, one outcome has been the construction of a completely new course on the teaching of reading, staffed by a team of tutors for whom this will be a major commitment, independent of their departmental work.

*In-service training*
The reading centre is also open by arrangement during the evenings every week from Monday to Thursday and since October 1970 over five thousand visits have been made to it by teachers in service. In each instance, the teachers indicate on what evening they wish to come and what materials or equipment or approach they want to examine and discuss. The centre has been used with teachers in a number of ways. First, for display material. The availability of such resources relevant to all stages of the primary school and the facility of handling series and schemes in their entirety, together with the chance to discuss their use with an experienced tutor, have already made considerable visible impact in the schools of south-west Scotland. Requisition, for instance, has become for many a more informed and selective process.

Second, the centre is used as a meeting place. For example, seminar groups of all Ayrshire teachers using or considering using ita met with the primary adviser to discuss the benefits and difficulties that arise from using the new medium. Also, primary advisers and teachers involved in the Craigie College language project 'The sea' considered aspects of their work with the project director.

The centre is also used as a venue for courses. Work with teachers has shown clearly the kind of in-service course content teachers want and where the real needs of the teacher lie. Emphasis therefore, throughout courses organized at the centre, has been on the practical involvement of the teachers in making equipment for use in their classrooms. All materials made are tried out in school and the results fed back for discussion at later meetings.

Recently workshops have been organized on such topics as 'Pre-reading materials', 'Aids to word recognition', 'Phonics in the classroom', 'Remedial materials and techniques' and 'The tape recorder as a reading aid'. Although these ventures were experimental, the response was outstanding. The teachers worked with considerable enthusiasm and the results achieved were impressive.

Longer courses, over periods of five to eight weeks, have dealt with broader topics including 'Improving reading skills', and 'Remedial reading: Techniques and materials'.

It is perhaps worth mentioning that teachers in service have been contributing constant feedback to the reading centre in a number of interesting areas, especially the use of the newer reading schemes. *Dominoes* (Oliver and Boyd), or the response to new approaches, ita, *Breakthrough to Literacy* or simply the reactions of children to series, such as Macmillan's *Nippers*, to television programmes like *Look and Read*, *Words and Pictures* and *It's Fun to Read*.

The undoubted success of the reading centre even in its brief two years of existence points to an even more profitable future for it, but not as an isolated facility in the college. We hope that in the course of the next few years the centre will become part of a curriculum development centre which will be producing learning resources for all stages of the primary school.

# 18   Television and the teaching of reading

*John E. Merritt*

In Open University courses, television, radio, correspondence texts and tutors provide a multimedia approach to teaching. Each medium has its own strengths and, of course, its own weaknesses. Our first consideration, therefore, in designing a course, is to try to use each medium to its best advantage. In doing so, we must depend to a large extent on personal judgment rather than on evidence. The content of each course is unique and no single course could justify the expenditure of large sums of money in order to establish what each medium could do best, or what kind of 'mix' might provide optimal results. It is very doubtful, in fact, whether even the most massive research programme would produce results any more conclusive than those of other researches into teaching in general, or into the teaching of reading in particular.

Our decisions, then, are based on an analysis of what we are trying to achieve and a fairly commonsense approach to decisions about what medium to use for what purpose. The purpose of the Reading Development course is to achieve changes—for the better, we hope—in the teaching of reading. We are concerned, in other words, with changes in behaviour. It is not our intention, however, to prescribe what these changes should be. Rather are we concerned to present a variety of studies which will enable the student to arrive at his own decisions as to what changes he wants to make in his own teaching. Our uses of the media must be designed to achieve such changes.

Any changes that are to be made in the classroom should only be made, in my view, if they can be justified in two ways: first, they must be based on sound theoretical principles; and second, the teacher must feel intuitively that what he is doing is right for the children for whom he is responsible. Next, changes can only be expected if the teacher feels that the proposed changes can, in practice, be brought about and that they are likely to help rather than interfere with his other curriculum activities. He must also be given some grounds for confidence that he, personally, could cope, i.e. that the proposed changes lie within his competence, and that if he introduced such changes, they would bring about the kinds of effect he desired.

These considerations now suggest ways in which the different media might be used. The study of theory might possibly be helped by a lecture type of programme on television or radio. However, the printed text must obviously carry the major burden for this aspect. Theory, however, is best understood when related to concrete examples and this is where television and radio can be used to particular advantage. The student, having studied his theory and engaged in certain practical activities, can be asked to note in the broadcast each theoretical principle exemplified. For example, listening to a teacher interacting with pupils who have read, or are going to read, a particular text, provides an excellent opportunity to note the effects of asking particular kinds of questions. Again, in a television programme, students may see pupils crossquestion an American visitor on differences between the presentation of particular items of news in American and British newspapers, and historical events in American and British textbooks. This provides an opportunity for noting the development of comprehension at the level of evaluation—and the level of interpretation, too, no doubt.

In attending to these issues, the student is able, at the same time, to gain insights into the quality of the processes presented. He can develop his own 'gut reaction'. He may intuitively reject completely what he sees—or he may reject what he sees but recognize that, done in his own way, there is something to be followed up in practice. Or he may see, accept, and apply. Hopefully, students will modify a great deal; everything must be adapted to some extent so that it fits the student's own teaching style and the particular needs of his pupils. The fact that work is presented on television or radio means, of course, that it has necessarily taken place, i.e. it must work. Unfortunately, we cannot give full weight in terms of broadcast time to all the various difficulties. Some will be included, however, as we wish to give some insight into problems—not slick solutions. The student can, in these circumstances, gain at least some understanding of how various kinds of procedure may be arranged and how they operate in practice.

He can also form some preliminary judgment of how he personally might cope in a similar situation. Here, care is taken to show teachers coping imperfectly from time to time so that the student recognizes that what is being demonstrated is not merely a procedure for paragons. We all fluctuate in our teaching—getting something just right one minute and making some elementary mistake the next. The teachers we show will be absolutely normal in this respect. They, and the student, will benefit from noting all the points of excellence, and pointers to improvements that could be made.

These illustrations are not complete; nevertheless, they probably give a fair picture of the kind of consideration that has aided judgment about the role of the correspondence text, television and radio.

So far, no mention has been made of the tutor. This will certainly not include direct instruction: the tutor's role is that of encouraging groups of students to share their experiences, their insights and their problems. Education is one of those areas where we can gain something from another person and both be enriched in the process. If the course is to produce real advances in the teaching of reading, it will be as a result of sharing experiences in this way.

The few available hours of tutorial time will not, however, suffice for this purpose. It is hoped, therefore, that students will get together in self-help groups at regular intervals throughout the course, and thereafter. Some of their activities will provide material worth presenting at meetings of local councils of UKRA—and perhaps at meetings of other professional associations. As each successive wave of students completes the course so, we hope, the studies begun will lead to investigations in greater depth in many areas too long neglected both in this country and abroad. The course, therefore, must be seen as only a starting point for the serious student of reading, although it will in itself make a significant contribution to the teaching of reading in this country.

But what of content? The number of courses on reading in an American university can run into double figures. We have only 170 hours of student time.

Our choice, we decided, lay between three broad areas—early stages of reading, developmental reading and remedial reading. Remedial reading was quickly dropped. We felt that attention to prevention was more important than cure at this stage. Early stages of reading was dismissed next. The need here is great: but there are many short courses on this aspect, as well as a considerable home-produced literature and an abundance of teaching material. Much still needs to be done to bring about improved standards of teaching in the early years. Nevertheless, the most serious deficit seemed to lie in the field of developmental reading. Every infant teacher knows she has to teach reading. Far too few teachers after that stage realize that there is anything to be done— they believe that anything to do with reading after the infant years is essentially 'remedial'.

We decided to concentrate on the middle years of schooling. The later years would have to wait their turn. We recognize, of course, that many teachers in infant schools and in remedial services will take this course. For them, the course provides a broad basis for later specialization, with opportunities to engage in a substantial study in areas of their choice. In addition, two units, i.e. twenty student hours, are devoted to each of these aspects. (This time should be compared with the amount of time devoted to these areas in courses of initial training.) Broadly, however, we are concerned with problems of the following kind:

1  What are the reading needs of the adult?
2  What are the reading needs of children?
3  Are the standards of reading of adults at all social and ability levels as high as they might be?

4   Are the standards of reading of children at all ability levels as high as they might be?
5   Do adult reading habits reflect a reasonable level of literacy and culture?
6   Do children's reading habits reflect a reasonable level of literacy and culture?
7   What implications do our answers have for the various kinds of reading that might be developed in the curriculum of the middle years of schooling?
8   What implications do our answers have for the development of reading skills in the middle years of schooling?
9   How may improvements be effected? And here, although we are primarily concerned with problems of curriculum organization and of method, we are also concerned with the extended professional role of the teacher, i.e. his role *vis à vis* colleagues, parents, professional associations, and so on.

Finally, it seems obvious that anyone who wishes to teach in a particular area should seek to improve his own personal competence in that area. Opportunities are therefore provided for the students to develop their own reading skills—to analyse their own reading habits and to seek to improve their own skills. In providing these activities, we hope to provide the student with additional insights which he can then transmit to his own pupils.

Who in this country, or indeed elsewhere, can provide a course such as I have described? Certain areas are well defined already and many people from either side of the Atlantic could provide what is necessary as a matter of course. Other areas draw heavily on American experience. But some areas are breaking new ground. Here, we can simply outline the problem as we see it and indicate the kinds of approach that seem most likely to lead to possible solutions. In these areas, we hope that many of our students will be willing to go beyond the work we set and, over a period of time, make a major contribution to reading theory and practice. These chances will be greater given the support of this Association.

# The contributors

BAMBERGER, Richard, Ph.D
Professor and Director of The International Institute for Children's and Juvenile Literature, Vienna

CARRILLO, Lawrence W., B.Sc., M.S., Ed.D.
Professor of Education, San Francisco State College, California, USA

CLARK, Margaret M., MA, Ed.B., Ph.D, F.B.Ps.S.
Senior Lecturer in Psychology, University of Strathclyde, Glasgow

FELDMANN, Shirley C., Ph.D.
Associate Professor, School of Education, The City College of the City University of New York, USA

GATHERER, William A., MA, Ph.D
HM Inspector of Schools, Edinburgh

GREDLER, Gilbert R., Ph.D
Chairman, Department of School Psychology, Temple University, Philadelphia, USA

HARDY, Madeline I., B.Sc., Ed.D.
Professor, Althouse College of Education, University of Western Ontario, Canada

HENDRY, T. Alastair, MA
Lecturer in Primary Education, Craigie College of Education, Ayr

LATHAM, William, B.Sc.
Principal Lecturer in Education, Totley-Thornbridge College of Education, Sheffield

LITTLE, Alan, Ph.D, JP
Head of the Reference Division, Community Relations Commission, London

MERRITT, John E., BA, A.B.Ps.S.
Professor of Educational Studies, The Open University, Bletchley, Buckinghamshire

McINNES, John, BA, M.Ed., Ed.D.
Associate Professor, Ontario Institute for Studies in Education, Canada

MORRIS, John G., MA, M.Ed.
Adviser in Research to Scottish Education Department, Edinburgh

MORRIS, Joyce M., BA, Ph.D
Language Arts Consultant, London

PETERS, Margaret L., MA, Ph.D
   Tutor in Primary Education, Cambridge Institute of Education
REID, Jessie, F., MA, M.Ed.
   Lecturer in Educational Sciences, University of Edinburgh
SOUTHGATE, Vera, B.Com. Dip.Psych, MA
   Senior Lecturer in Curriculum Studies, School of Education,
   University of Manchester
WIJK, Axel M., Ph.D
   Reader in English (retired), University of Stockholm
WOODS, Janet, BA, MA
   Senior Research Worker, Inner London Education Authority